THE BATTLE

Within

what being a mom taught me about myself

J. Robin Wood

journeyforth®

Greenville, South Carolina

Library of Congress Cataloging-in Publication Data
Wood, J. Robin, date.
  The battle within : what being a mom taught me about myself /
J. Robin Wood.
     pages cm
  Includes bibliographical references.
  ISBN 978-1-60682-967-7 (perfect bound pbk. : alk. paper)—
ISBN 978-1-60682-968-4 (ebook) 1. Mothers—Religious life.
2. Motherhood—Religious aspects—Christianity. I. Title.
  BV4529.18.W66 2015
  248.8'431—dc23
                                                    2014031398

Cover photo: iStockphoto.com © BrianAJackson (heart-shaped hole)

All Scripture is quoted from the King James Version. Words or phrases in bold represent the author's emphasis.

The fact that materials produced by other publishers may be referred to in this volume does not constitute an endorsement of the content or theological position of materials produced by such publishers.

Design by Chris Taylor
Page layout by Michael Boone

© 2015 by BJU Press
Greenville, South Carolina 29614
JourneyForth Books is a division of BJU Press.

Printed in the United States of America

ISBN 978-1-60682-967-7
eISBN 978-1-60682-968-4

15 14 13 12 11 10 9 8 7 6 5 4 3 2 1

To my parents
Terry and Joyce Sisney,
who taught me early to love and respect the word of God

To Bobby,
who spoke Truth into my life when I was too tired to fight
and gave me hope

And to Cotter, Caeleigh, and Caeden,
who experienced my battles firsthand
and loved me anyway

ACKNOWLEDGMENTS

With sincere gratitude to my extended family and the precious friends and sisters of Norway Baptist Church, Faith Baptist Church, Northland Neighbors, Pioneer Christian School, and Harvest Baptist Church for their genuine love, faithful encouragement, constant prayers, helping hands, side-splitting humor, shared tears, and wise counsel during my early mom years. And to Nancy, my editor, who inspired, coached, guided, and prayed me through this project. I am eternally grateful.

Contents

From the Author

Dear Mom, my fellow soldier,

These chapters chronicle my fiercest spiritual battles as a new mother.

I was twenty-nine before God brought my husband, Bobby, and me together, and I had thoroughly enjoyed my seven years of full-time ministry as a single woman. Our first son was born fifteen months after our wedding. Another sixteen months later, God blessed our home with twins—a son and a daughter. During the first three years of our marriage, we also moved four times, Bobby pursued his PhD, and we joined a full-time ministry. These blessings and challenges combined to set the stage for many battles between my flesh and my spirit. I must confess that my flesh was skillful in attacking me, and time after time I clung to the edge of spiritual failure and despair.

For years I had greatly anticipated the day I would become a wife and mother and surrender the majority of my outside ministries and interests for the sake of my husband and children, but the reality of living my dream left me disillusioned and resentful. The glow of new motherhood quickly faded into a desperate struggle for survival. My ideals evaporated with the shrill sound of babies crying in the night and three stinky bottoms in need of constant diaper changes. And the laundry, oh the laundry.

I am convinced that marriage and motherhood are extreme tests of selflessness. I am also convinced that every woman who enters these responsibilities is unprepared for the extent of the selflessness required, and that we are doomed to failure if we try to succeed by ourselves, in our own strength, and for our own happiness.

But there is hope—an absolutely rock-solid truth. God is faithful. His Word is powerful and full of comfort. And there is help—real, credible support.

We have everything we need in His Word and through His Spirit to defeat the power of our personal Supermom—our own sinful nature.

God's Word is alive. It's true. It's without error and can be trusted because of its author—God Himself. When you come to the passages of God's Word in this book, please take time to read them word for word. Resist the temptation to skip them or to skim over them lightly. Nothing I say in these pages even compares to the powerful Word of God, so please slow down and focus on the verses, no matter how familiar they are to you. You'll find some verses repeated. God's Word is beautifully applicable to every battle we face.

Please remember this book is a record of *my* struggles with my sin nature and how the powerful Word of God is giving me victory. Your struggles may be similar, or they may be different. There are questions at the end of each chapter to help you identify Supermom's attacks in your heart and battle-plan verses from the Bible to help you conquer her temptations.

It is my prayer that this journal of my struggle and these battle plans will encourage you who are in the trenches of motherhood with me, and that together we will emerge from our battlefields triumphant and thankful that the cross of Jesus changes us, that His grace transforms us, and that His Word is the Truth that sets us free.

To the Triumph of Grace,
J. Robin Wood

The arm of flesh will fail you,
Ye dare not trust your own.[1]

George Duffield, Jr.

Chapter One
Supermom Exposed

Supermom is the stuff dreams are made of. She's the woman with multiple children who doesn't look like she's had any. She's the homemaker with a clean house, clean laundry, and a clean minivan (even the pockets are free of petrified French fries and sticky crumbs). She knows all the answers, takes time for everyone, supports her husband in his work and ministry, and still has an amazing devotional life. In her spare time, she manages to bring in a steady income to the family budget. She's the mom who is creative, innovative, frugal, and generous.

Her children are obedient, well-mannered, unselfish, and clean. She cooks for the widows, the sick, and the shut-ins, and still treats her family to Southern Living-style meals on a regular basis. She runs the church nursery, gives piano lessons, volunteers in the community association, and carpools for Little League soccer. She exercises daily and runs at least one marathon every year. She is a motivator, a maverick, a mystery.

She's the woman we always wanted to be. She's the woman we're sure our husbands wish they had married. She's the woman whose standard of excellence we know we will never attain.

We fear her. We respect her. We hate her. We secretly suspect she must be related to that other elusive biblical female, the Proverbs 31 Woman.

I've come to believe there is a Supermom who lives in each one of us. She hangs over our heads, making us feel guilty for feeding the kids peanut butter sandwiches for lunch the third . . . make that the sixth day in a row. She raises her eyebrow when we don't clean the floor behind the toilet or when we stuff dirty laundry under the bed before company arrives. She frowns in disgust when we compare our skirt size to other women in the room and come up with the highest number. We allow her to criticize us, chastise us, judge us, and manipulate us.

Her influence is strong. And it is deadly.

If you let her, she will deceive you into focusing on appearances. She will keep you so busy trying to look good that you will neglect your husband and children. She will scream at you when you fail her, and she will condemn you when you damage her reputation. She will delude you into pursuing the wrong priorities and then mask your selfishness from your own eyes.

When you fulfill her expectations, she will pacify you with the praise of people and fill your head with pride in yourself. She will tempt you to become critical of others who have not attained the level of Supermom status to which you have risen. Then she will betray you and let you fall.

She is your sinful human nature. And she is your enemy.

THE ENEMY WITHIN

We were all born with our sinful natures—our natural bent toward selfishness and pride. It's an integral part of us, touching everything we think, feel, do, and are. We don't automatically turn our hearts towards God. In fact the reality is just the opposite. Our sinful natures hate God and reject His authority in our lives. We argue with God, question His character, and are sure that we could do a better job of running our corner of the universe given the chance.

The Bible has much to say about our natural, sinful state.

> *There is none righteous, no not one: There is none that understandeth, there is none that seeketh after God. . . . there is none that doeth good, no, not one. (Romans 3:10–12)*

> *For all have sinned and come short of the glory of God. (Romans 3:23)*

And because of our sins, we deserve eternal punishment.

> *For the wages of sin is death. (Romans 6:23a)*

But God loved us through no merit of our own. He not only says that He loves us, but He has already acted on this amazing love for people who reject Him.

> *But God commendeth his love toward us, in that, while we were yet sinners, Christ died for us. (Romans 5:8)*

He gave His son, Jesus, to die for our sins upon a cross so that we are covered in Christ's righteousness and have a place in heaven for eternity at His side.

> *The gift of God is eternal life through Jesus Christ our Lord. (Romans 6:23b)*

So if you've accepted God's gift of salvation through His Son, Jesus Christ, your eternity is something you can anticipate with joy! I sure do. I long for that day when I see my Savior, when I'm free from my sinful nature, and when this war is over.

But what about the time between now and then? Eternally speaking, our lives may be short, but seriously, as a mom, some days just feel like an eternity. We can't avoid walking through some dark valleys and thorny pathways here on earth. Valleys are actually designed by God for us for our good and ultimately for His glory. And although we have the Holy Spirit living within us, every Christian mom knows we are in a critical daily spiritual battle—the battle between right and wrong. The Apostle Paul warns us that "the flesh lusteth against the Spirit, and the Spirit against the flesh: and these are contrary the one to the other: so that ye cannot do the things that ye would" (Galatians 5:17).

He implores us to "put on the whole armour of God, that ye may be able to stand against the wiles of the devil. For we wrestle not against flesh and blood, but against principalities, against powers, against the rulers of the darkness of this world, against spiritual wickedness in high places" (Ephesians 6:11–12).

You and I know this battle is real. We fight it every day and through many long nights. It is a battle for authority, and it rages between the Holy Spirit in our lives and our sinful, fleshly nature. I have named my sinful nature "Supermom."

The truth is we either submit our spirits to the authority of the Holy Spirit or to the authority of Supermom, minute by minute, sometimes even second by second.

We know that we can't fight the battle alone. I've tried that and failed miserably. You probably have too.

> *For I know that in me (that is, in my flesh,) dwelleth no good thing: for to will is present with me; but how to perform that which is good I find not. For the good that I would I do not: but the evil which I would not, that I do. (Romans 7:18–19)*

We need the Holy Spirit. We need the power and wisdom of God's Word to fight Supermom.

Supermom has many weapons. She uses our thoughts, our emotions, our hopes, our circumstances, and even the very people we love to try to drive us away from God. She is deeply wicked and ultimately desires to destroy us.

The Bible says that I should be showing Christ in the way I mother my children. It says that because God has forgiven my sin, I have been given the Holy Spirit to help me live in victory over Supermom every single day. God tells me to "walk in the Spirit, and ye shall not fulfill the lust of the flesh" (Galatians 5:16).

FAKE FRUIT

I don't want to be a sinful mom wrapped up in myself. I want my kids to see Jesus real and alive in my life. So to be that kind of person, I *must* walk in the Spirit. I must day by day, minute by minute be submissive to the Spirit's work in my heart. Seriously, that *sounds* easy. It's easy to say. It's easy to read. It's easy to counsel others to do.

But actually doing it? How exactly do I walk in the Spirit when I'm up to my neck in dirty laundry and my toddlers' non-stop whining makes me want to scream? And what does a mom who is walking in the Spirit actually look like?

Further down in Galatians 5, God enlightens us to His good plan for us.

> But the fruit of the Spirit is love, joy, peace,
> longsuffering, gentleness, goodness, faith, meekness,
> temperance. (Galatians 5:22–23)

Oh, great. A mom who walks in the Spirit is pretty much perfect. *Sigh. Grumble.* My kids would probably tell you I'm unrelated to her.

When I asked God to save me from Supermom's stranglehold on me and to help me be a mom who reflected Christ to my children, He gave me these verses—the verses about the fruit of the Spirit that should be in my life. And they didn't exactly warm my heart. They actually irritated me—spiritually.

Now it's time for a confession. These verses almost sounded like a horrific divine to-do list. I felt like it said, "Okay, Robin, be loving to your selfish, disobedient children. Be joyful when you soak diarrhea out of the sheets. Force yourself to be patient when your daughter ruins her Sunday clothes with a red marker on the way to church. Make your voice gentle to your son after he plasters his sister's hair with Vaseline. Humbly keep your house clean for unexpected drop-in guests." And the list goes on.

Being the to-do list kind of girl that I am, I took right to this challenge. I pulled my exhausted self up by my shabby flip-flops, stirred up my gumption, and got to it. I took a different fruit of the Spirit each week and valiantly, desperately tried to show my children a mom who "walked in the Spirit." And what a failure I was. Over and over and over.

Remember those verses in John 15 where Jesus is telling his disciples that they should bear much fruit? It was familiar to me. I'd read it before. He says "I am the vine, ye are the branches: He that abideth in me, and I in him, the same bringeth forth much fruit: for without me ye can do nothing. . . . Herein is my Father glorified, that ye bear much fruit" (John 15:5 and 8).

I worked so hard to produce that fruit! I purposely focused on these characteristics of the Spirit and tried to force each one out on my visible life "branch" for all to see. And all I got was cheap plastic imitations that stuck on me temporarily and wilted at the first sign of stress unless they blew completely off in a typhoon of emotion. The scary thing was, even my toddlers knew the difference between fake and real fruit. What was going wrong?

I was completely, utterly defeated. My discouragement overwhelmed me at times. I had some dark days when my mind was so twisted by my sin I couldn't think straight. I was miserable. And my family suffered for it too.

And then one very dark dreary day in February, buried in snow in the north woods of Wisconsin, God brought me back once again to those familiar verses in John 15. And I read them again, but found I had completely missed the obvious.

> *I am the vine, ye are the branches: He that abideth*
> *in me, and I in him, the same bringeth forth much*
> *fruit: for without me ye can do nothing. (John*
> *15:5)*

I felt guilty. How dumb was I? Obviously I was not doing a good job being like Jesus in my home, but this verse told me it was because I wasn't *abiding* in Him in the first place. I didn't question my salvation from sin. I knew I was a child of God, saved from the consequences of my sin by His forgiveness and through the power of His blood shed for me. But I realized my understanding of what it meant to actually abide in Christ was completely skewed. If I was a child of God, why wasn't I bearing the fruit that comes from Christ? The answer came in John 15:4.

> *Abide in me, and I in you. As the branch cannot*
> *bear fruit of itself, except it abide in the vine; no*
> *more can ye, except ye abide in me.*

I had my aha moment then. I couldn't get real love, joy, peace, and all the rest of the real crop by myself. No herculean effort by Supermom could produce the real thing. And if I had failed so far, then it was because Supermom was trying to grow the fruit. And Supermom was evil.

Don't get me wrong. This wasn't a new concept to me. I knew all the verses about doing all things in His strength and for His glory. I even had opportunities to counsel others to do the same.

Except I had never really applied it to myself as a mother. And, until now, I had never fully understood the depth of my sin, the complete inadequacy of my efforts, or the utter futility of trying to be a Christian mom without resting in Christ.

Somewhere along the way, I had bought in to the lofty and completely arrogant idea that as a Christian mom my ultimate goal was to be Supermom. After all, I want to be a good testimony. I want to be faithful. I want to be the very best mom I can be. I want to *be* Supermom!

Is that so bad? Is there really anything wrong with that? Yep. Supermom had blinded me to my selfish motivation. I wanted to be Supermom because I wanted to do a good job, to feel successful as a parent, to feel good about myself, to be someone other moms could look up to, to have children that reflected well on me. I wanted others to see my spirituality and be in awe of my relationship with God. Oh, the deceptive ways of Supermom!

Confessing my blindness to the sinful inner workings of my own heart is where I had to start. I had to see my sin for the horrible sickness that it is. Being humbled by the Word of God is a painfully personal experience that leaves you feeling raw and exposed—even bleeding at times. Seeing my sin through the eyes of God was humbling indeed.

Confessing my sin came next. I confessed my pride, my selfishness, and my complete failure to be a successful mom in God's eyes. But most of all, I confessed my failure to bear real fruit because my prideful confidence in myself kept me from full dependence on Christ. I was too busy trying to do my good work my way.

That was a breaking point for me, the turning point in my momhood. Am I going to be a mom who abides in Christ? Or will I continue to just try harder to do my best?

When my kids grow up and leave my house, will they remember me for the meals I fixed them? For the clean house they lived in? For the activities and opportunities I gave them? For the clothes they wore?

Or will they remember me as a mom who knew my sinful bent and was completely dependent on God for my existence and for the patience to answer their thousand questions? Who daily showed them God's love by putting aside my to-do list in order to focus on the important happenings in their lives no matter how insignificant they might seem to me? Who asked them for their forgiveness when I responded selfishly? Who taught them by open, transparent, humble example to solve problems God's way? Who choose God's glory over my own?

Will they remember me as Supermom? Or will they remember God in me?

These questions stirred me. They called me to learn to abide in Christ and to understand the depth of my depravity and my utter dependence on God. They set me on a journey to identify and bring down the strongholds of Supermom in my life.

God's desire for us is that we abide in Him, know Him, bear His fruit, and become reflectors of Christ. He wants to love us. He wants us to love Him. Nothing in His desire mentions us being Supermoms. Isn't that a relief?

Christian sister, you are not alone in your battle with Supermom. I'm right there with you, struggling with my sin too, along with countless other Christian moms around you. This book is a reflection of my journey. It is soul-baringly honest.

And it is painful at times. It's the record of my ugly battles with Supermom.

I don't want you to be deceived here. These pages aren't going to give you the quick-fix strategies to become a perfect mom. This book won't tell you how to raise perfect kids or keep a clean house or lose those baby pounds. They also don't glorify my sin or make excuses for the wickedness in my heart.

These pages hold a simple battle plan against Supermom, the sinful nature we each carry with us in our human bodies.

God has demanded my honesty in sharing with you this part of my journey toward being a mom who passionately loves Christ, and these pages will magnify the powerful Word of God that has begun that work in my heart.

WHAT ABOUT ME?

1. Am I a daughter of the King? Have I accepted God's gift of the complete sacrifice of Jesus on the cross as payment for my sin?

   No amount of good works can ever make us right with a holy God.

   For by grace are ye saved through faith; and that not of yourselves: it is the gift of God: Not of works, lest any man should boast. (Ephesians 2:8–9)

2. As a daughter of the King, how aware am I of the daily battle that is still going on in my heart? It's not a battle for my eternal destiny; that has already been decided. The battle now is between the Holy Spirit and my sinful heart—Supermom—and it's a battle for who will have the authority over my life.

   - In what areas of my life do I have conflict? In relationships with people? In circumstances that seem beyond my control? In medical or physical difficulties? Write them out. Be honest.

   - Remember that Supermom is masterfully deceptive. Many, many times what seems like conflict with someone or something else in my life is actually a cleverly cloaked battle initiated by Supermom and between her and the Holy Spirit.

3. Remember that Supermom will use anything she can to get you to sin, to steal glory from God, and to be generally powerless as a daughter of the King. She loves to mock Him. Look at the list of your conflicts. Take the time to consider each and answer the following questions:

- In this conflict, how can I bring glory to God?

- In this conflict, how can I bring glory to myself?

- In this conflict, who is winning right now?

Leave no unguarded place,
No weakness of the soul;
Take every virtue, every grace,
And fortify the whole.

From strength to strength go on,
Wrestle and fight and pray;
Tread all the powers of darkness down,
And win the well-fought day.[1]

Charles Wesley

Chapter Two
The Battle for My Mind

I have put off writing this chapter for months. Actually, for years. I've known in my heart God wanted me to write it, but my flesh balked, dragged its feet, and outright rebelled. "It's too personal. It's too scary. No other mom will understand this," Supermom told me. "You're a really bad mom, and you need to protect your reputation and shield yourself from others discovering just how bad you are."

But God convicted my mind with a gem of truth from my grad-school days. I'll never forget a wise instructor who told us one of our sin nature's tactics is to get us to think we're alone, that somehow our problem is exceptional, and that because of the uniqueness of our bad situation, we're somehow excused from the sinful attitudes and behaviors we therefore display. We're victims and just can't help what happens. These are all very sweet lies of Supermom I wanted so badly to believe.

But God reminded me that "there hath no temptation taken you but such as is common to man: but God is faithful, who will not suffer you to be tempted above that ye are able; but will with the temptation also make a way to escape, that ye may be able to bear it" (1 Corinthians 10:13).

REALITIES

This is the story of the battle for my mind.

Looking back, I believe one of the most bittersweet realities of my early momhood was the privilege of living continually at the end of my self—bitter because I had to face my human weakness and bent toward pride; sweet because God carried my spirit through those dark days personally. I was completely dependent on Him *spiritually*. But that part wasn't actually new to me.

What was new to me was the complete dependence on Him *physically*, *mentally*, and *emotionally*. His grace pulled my mind to "think Bible." Even the days when I could not find the time to meet with God in silence alone, His Word spoke to my mind. Yes, I confess to you, I didn't always have formal "devotions" alone with God every day in my early momhood years.

I also confess to you that sometimes when I *did* spend time alone with God, it was pretty short and usually interrupted by an ear-splitting cry or some household chore. I remember that I almost always was mentally distracted by the to-do list screaming in my head or the physical exhaustion of my body that allowed my mind to wander or completely shut down. Sometimes I'd read my Bible for five minutes and realize suddenly that I had no idea what I had just read. I didn't have a disciplined Bible study regimen in those days. I was in survivor mode most of the time, desperately, even selfishly, grabbing at the promises from my God that would help me make it through the day. I know you relate.

Back then—for several years in fact—the most exciting time of my day was sleeping. I craved it; I looked forward to it; I missed it. And since I'm admitting my faults to you right now, I'll just go ahead and tell you that most days I craved sleep more than time alone with God.

This reality of my human frailty scared me. What had happened to me? Wasn't I a Christian? Had God forsaken me? Was I a terrible mom after all? Why couldn't I just handle this?

I resented my human weakness. Supermom told me I was better than this failure I had become. I was married to a wonderful Christian man; I had a counseling degree; I knew the answers. I could just depend on my common sense and God-given abilities to cope. She told me that I just needed to try harder, be more disciplined, nag my husband to do more to help me out, and make excuses for myself. I had three kids under the age of two, and my husband was gone most of the time, for heaven's sake!

She wanted me to do anything but see myself for who I really was: a weak woman completely dependent on God for her very next breath, completely dependent on God to keep her from going insane, and completely dependent on God for wisdom to relate to her children.

Completely dependent.

Supermom hates that. It goes against her very core. Supermom is all about herself. She doesn't need anyone else. She doesn't need God. She *can* handle it. She can make it all happen. She can survive.

Supermom isn't the dependent type because she wants all the praise and glory for what she's accomplished. She doesn't want to share that success with anyone. Especially not God.

I felt like I had been grabbed by Giant Despair, the master of Doubting Castle (who was surely a relative of Supermom) in *The Pilgrim's Progress* and that he had thrown me in his dungeon with his other prisoners intent on my destruction. I could hear Supermom taunting me in my mind, offering me ideas for my escape from my weakness, from my failure.

There were days when I think I really did hover at the edge of desperation and depression. Days when I couldn't see any light at the end of the tunnel. Days of no hope. Dark days when I considered fleeting incomprehensible thoughts. Days when Supermom whispered sinful, scary questions in my head like, "Since you turned out to be such a failure at being a mom, wouldn't it just be better to end it all?" and "Don't you think your children deserve a better mom than you could ever be?" and "Don't you think Bobby deserves a better wife than you are?" "What would happen if you just ended your misery? Then Bobby could find someone else to raise his children—someone much better qualified to do the job. . . ."

I told you this was ugly.

In my discouragement, she whispered, "But your children are part of you and have your same nature, so they're flawed too. There's a chance they won't amount to much either." And the darkest thought of all, "Wouldn't it just be better for Bobby if you and the kids were out of his life altogether? Then he could do his ministry unhampered by your failure."

In my rested moments, I was overwhelmed with a deep sense of shame. I dearly loved my husband! I dearly loved my children! They were precious gifts from God. I was so thankful for them. But then Supermom would jump in with her thoughts. "That's just it," she would whisper. "They are gifts from God, and they obviously deserve better than you."

I'll never forget the clarifying day when I suddenly understood the thought process that brought Andrea Yates, the Texas mom who purposefully drowned her children, to her breaking point. And it horribly scared me. When she committed that unspeakable crime, I was a young, single Christian schoolteacher. It broke my heart, and it outraged me. How could any mother kill her own children? What could possess her to do such a horrible thing? How did she get to that point where she could mentally justify murder?

Now I knew. She had come to the end of herself and then she listened to the voices of Supermom in her head. She had no hope within herself. She didn't take the Word of God and fight back. And finally, after feeling like a failure for so long, after feeling like her life was out of her control, the voices made sense. *Remove the problem, and life will get better.* The only thing was that the problem wasn't rooted in her children. My problem wasn't rooted in my children or my husband or circumstances either. Andrea wanted some form of control over her life, and I did too.

When asked by authorities for the reason she killed her children, Andrea replied, "Because I'm a bad mother." Andrea chose to listen to her sinful nature rather than the Word of God. The battle was fought. Andrea didn't choose the right weapon, and she lost.

And now in the north woods of Wisconsin buried in snow, I was faced with the same choice. A key reason God gave me children, it appeared, was to shine the spotlight on my sinful nature. I clearly remember realizing that I wasn't insane, and I wasn't sick. I was very simply and horribly sinful.

THE BATTLE

This was the battle between my sinful nature and the Spirit of God within me. This was the battle to give either Supermom or the Spirit control of my mind. And I could choose the outcome.

So would I listen to Supermom whisper possible solutions in my ear of how to regain control of my life? She was wrong, of course! But in my physical, mental, and spiritual exhaustion, her ideas of control seemed somehow plausible, and I was tempted. I was tempted for about a week. They were just fleeting thoughts of despair, yes, but they were real. And I confess to you that from time to time in my despair, I entertained them.

Supermom, my sinful nature, was waging war against me, not because of me or because I'm so special, but because she hates God, and I'm His beloved child.

And she's not stupid. She knew well that the best time to strike her enemy is when she's already weak. My tired physical state was a key factor in her attack. She also knew to wait until my husband, my best friend, was out of town on a ministry trip, so I would be alone, so I would be even more tired with no relief or help with the children in the evenings and nights. She knew that we lived far from the helping hands of family. She timed her attacks perfectly like the pro that she is.

Finally one evening, a major battle for my mind was fought.

Bobby was out of town. He had forgotten to call to check in on me that night, and my feelings were hurt. I felt forgotten, and I felt angry. I was struggling with a cold virus. The kids, ages two and three at the time, had been exceptionally challenging that day being in the throes of potty training. The house was a wreck and smelled less than fresh. I had lost my temper on more than one occasion that day and was feeling guilty about it. I was tired. I was resentful of my state in life. And I had come to the sad realization that potty training, cleaning the house, or doing laundry would never, ever bring me any personal gratification or sense of accomplishment. I had worked hard from early in the morning until late at night doing apparently nothing. And I would have to do it all again the next day with no relief in sight. The conditions were perfect for Supermom's attack.

As I lay down in bed that night, I remember staring at the ceiling with glazed eyes, doubtful that I could even manage to drag my body from the bed to respond to their cries during the night.

And she attacked.

"Haven't you had enough yet? Your husband doesn't even care enough to check on you. He probably thinks you're a failure too. Your children are going to drain you of every ounce of being until you're dead anyway. What's the point? Your husband doesn't need you hindering him anymore. Your children deserve a better mother than you could ever be. You're a failure. Admit it. End this, and just be done with it."

I remember that out of sheer desperation from the bottom of a dark, black pit I whispered out loud, "God, help me!"

Instantly a piece of a verse came to mind like a distant life line. I spoke it out loud.

> *Thou wilt keep him in perfect peace, whose mind*
> *is stayed on thee. (Isaiah 26:3)*

And another verse spoken out loud.

Fear thou not; for I am with thee: be not dismayed; for I am thy God: I will strengthen thee; yea, I will help thee. (Isaiah 41:10)

A holy fury overtook me. I jumped out of my bed and started pacing back and forth talking out loud to my sinful heart. Yelling at her.

Get thee behind me, Satan. (Luke 4:8)

Trust in the Lord with all thine heart; and lean not unto thine own understanding. (Proverbs 3:5)

Being confident of this very thing, that he which hath begun a good work in you will perform it until the day of Jesus Christ. (Philippians 1:6)

Yea, though I walk through the valley of death, I will fear no evil: for thou art with me. (Psalm 23:4)

For God hath not given us the spirit of fear; but of power, and of love, and of a sound mind. (2 Timothy 1:7)

I remember that as I quoted verses out loud to myself—to Supermom—, I actually felt the spiritual and physical strength God promises to His children in Isaiah 40:29–31 come over me.

He giveth power to the faint; and to them that have no might he increaseth strength. Even the youths shall faint and be weary, and the young men [young moms too!] shall utterly fall: But they that wait upon the Lord shall renew their strength; they shall mount up with wings as eagles; they shall run, and not be weary; and they shall walk, and not faint.

I grabbed my Bible and opened it. God took me to Ephesians 4:17–23 highlighting certain phrases to my heart.

*This I say therefore . . . that ye henceforth **walk not as other Gentiles walk,** in the vanity of* *their mind, having **the understanding dark-ened**, being alienated from the life of God through the **ignorance that is in them**, because of the **blindness of their heart**: who being past feeling have given themselves over. . . . **But ye have not so learned Christ; . . . and be renewed in the spirit of your mind**.*

I remember that I knelt beside my bed—okay, I actually fell on my knees. There was no careful kneeling. This was battle, and tears were everywhere.

And I confessed my sinful thoughts to God:

- Thoughts of despair and hopelessness

- Thoughts doubting God's goodness to me

- Thoughts of pride

- My desire to control my life and the people in it

- My selfish need to be admired and appreciated

- My thoughts of resentment toward God, toward my husband, and toward my children for not giving me what I thought I deserved

- My thoughts of failure, of anger, of bitterness

- My failure to keep my mind on Him

I confessed all of this. I asked for His forgiveness. And just like that, in the blink of an eye, He gave it. Freely. Completely. And His love filled my heart. Forgiven sin. Unconditional love.

My last conscious thought as I fell asleep that night was that God was with me and that He loved me more than I'd ever be able to comprehend on this earth. I felt overwhelmed by His love. My mind was at perfect peace.

The next morning my husband was still gone. The children were still challenging and still hadn't figured out what the toilet was for. No one came over and did my laundry for me or washed the dishes. I was still physically tired. And I still felt no personal gratification for anything I did that day. Nothing changed in my physical or emotional existence.

But my spirit was quiet and my mind was held in peace by God's love for me.

THIS IS WAR!

Throughout that week, He brought more verses to help me hold Supermom at bay.

> *Finally, brethren, whatsoever things are true,*
> *whatsoever things are honest, whatsoever things are*
> *just, whatsoever things are pure, whatsoever things*
> *are lovely, whatsoever things are of a good report;*
> *if there be any virtue, and if there be any praise,*
> *think on these things. (Philippians 4:8)*

> *For to be carnally minded is death; but to be spiri-*
> *tually minded is life and peace. (Romans 8:6)*

He reminded me that "though we walk in the flesh, we do not war after the flesh: (For the weapons of our warfare are not carnal, but mighty through God to the pulling down of strong holds;) Casting down imaginations, and every high thing that exalteth itself against the knowledge of God, and bringing into captivity every thought to the obedience of Christ" (2 Corinthians 10:3–5).

After reading these verses, I remember that it dawned on me that day that I had just waged a spiritual battle. I went to Ephesians 6:11–17, the passage about putting on the armor of God.

> *Put on the whole armour of God, that ye may be*
> *able to stand against the wiles of the devil. For we*
> *wrestle not against flesh and blood, but against*
> *principalities, against powers, against the rulers*
> *of the darkness of this world, against spiritual*
> *wickedness in high places. Wherefore take unto you*
> *the whole armour of God, that ye may be able to*
> *withstand in the evil day, and having done all,*

*to stand. Stand therefore, having your loins girt about with truth, and having on the breastplate of righteousness; And your feet shod with the preparation of the gospel of peace; **Above all, taking the shield of faith, wherewith ye shall be able to quench all the fiery darts of the wicked. And take the helmet of salvation, and the sword of the Spirit, which is the word of God.***

I read it with new eyes. This wasn't just a vague romantic picture of being a Christian anymore. Not to me. This passage had my sweat, tears, and spiritual blood on it. I had fought this battle.

I had seen the depth of my sin—my sin that still wanted to destroy me; my sin already forgiven by God through Jesus' death on the cross for me.

For me! I had always been grateful for my salvation and that I had asked for God's forgiveness as a child. Eternally, my sin was defeated and, according to Romans 8:38–39, nothing would ever separate me from God.

But now I knew I still had sin in my body in this flesh. Sin that needed to be confessed to God. I had just missed the depth of it and the breadth of it and the amazing way my sin permeated every fiber of my nature. I had gone through my Christian life in the grace of God, avoiding the "big sins," and maintaining my public testimony as a Christian woman. But I never stopped to understand and consider the horrible reality of my sinfulness.

And therefore I had never really grasped the thought of how amazing it is that a perfect, holy God would love me and that His love for me would drive Him to suffer personal loss and grief in the death of His only Son to allow me to fellowship with Him. What love!

My prayer for you, sister, is that God would bring you to a place where you have this amazing opportunity, that you would stop and be completely horrified by the depth of *your* sin, that God would grant you the wisdom to call sin in your life what it is, and that in understanding your sin, your spirit would also be overwhelmed at the unconditional love of your God for you.

My second prayer for you and me is that we would use our Swords daily in our battle with Supermom.

If you're a Christian, then you already possess every piece of this armor, as I did. But you must take up your shield of faith in your God by crying out to Him for help. I want you to see with your own spiritual eyes that your faith in God really *will* "quench all the fiery darts of the wicked" (Eph. 6:16), and I want you to see firsthand the power of the Sword God has given to us.

His Word works. You can do literal, out-loud battle with Supermom with it. And win!

You can never take up your Sword and lose. Crouching beneath your shield of faith isn't enough. You have to go on the offensive and *fight!*

As a Christian, I'm a soldier-mom in a spiritual battle. When confronted with the deep sin in my heart, I must pick up a weapon. The kicker, though, is that I can choose my weapon.

God loves us and, knowing the intense spiritual battle we're fighting, He gave us a weapon. Not just any weapon. It's a weapon that guarantees victory. Every time.

Seriously? Can you imagine the armed forces of our country having a weapon like this? If you possess a weapon that guarantees victory every time you use it, you'd be pretty foolish not to pick it up at the first sign of battle.

This is war. Don't ever think otherwise. Supermom is out to destroy us. She hates us with a seething hatred. But God has given us the weapon to defeat her. It's the same one Jesus used to resist Satan's temptations in the wilderness: God's Word.

This Word is alive. It's personal and it's meant to be used constantly to defeat the sin within us. It protects our minds; it repels Satan and his temptations; it comforts us; it reveals God to us; it convicts us of sin; and it conquers the sinful Supermom within us.

Pick up your Sword! Fight! *Never* give up!

DECEPTIVELY "GOOD"

In her scheme to express false concern to me, Supermom offered me a wide selection of possible solutions to whatever problem I was facing. She has an amazing array of options to choose from. She has answers when we need something to help us feel better about ourselves, our situation, and our crisis.

Sometimes she offers us a new habit.

- We might pick up stuff, developing an obsessive shopping addiction.

- We might pick up chocolate, feeding a food craving.

- We might bury ourselves in personal entertainment, keeping our minds busy so we don't see our sin.

- We might pick up a pill, dulling the pain of conviction with drugs.

- We might pick up a psychotherapist to explore the possibilities of who we can blame for our internal unrest.

- We can become professional blame shifters, blaming everyone and everything except our sin in our hearts.

- We can even pick up the victim cry, pointing our fingers and our voices to those who have wronged us, never seeing that we ourselves are in the sinking ship of bitterness.

Very often, Supermom cleverly offers us options cloaked in spirituality as well.

- We might pick up a variety of consuming ministries hoping to deaden our feelings of conviction by good deeds to others.

- We might join a ladies' Bible study and find ourselves caught in the seduction of studying God's Word impersonally.

- We might work on church projects with fervor and passion so that we can find satisfaction in the fact that everyone knows we have a heart for God's people.

- We might do a lot of good for a lot of people but do it all with a completely selfish motive.

And all the time, Supermom looks on with smug approval. She has succeeded when she keeps us from picking up God's Word to deal with her, the sin in our hearts. She has kept us from picking up our Sword, the *only* thing that will defeat her.

She can survive and even flourish when we remain on the defensive. But she cannot stand against His Word. If we pick up our Swords, she loses. If we go on the offensive, *we win.*

> *Resist the devil, and he will flee from you. (James 4:7)*

But how many of us are really good at doing this? I know so many dear sisters who live in defeat, not victory.

You know these women too. This world, our hospitals, our churches, our homes are filled with broken women who waged this spiritual battle and lost. You may be one of them. I was for a while. These women are professing Christians, but they never take up their Sword of the Spirit, the Word of God. You can't win without it. Don't ever think you're strong enough. Only God's Word has, can, and will continue to utterly defeat your sinful nature.

This is what 2 Corinthians 10:3–5 means when it tells us that the way we do battle is not the same way as those without Christ do battle. Everyone has conflict, and the world entices us with many choices for coping with that conflict within our minds. Look at those two lists again on the previous page.

But as Christians, our weapons are spiritual, and we are engaging in spiritual battle when we tear down any prideful way of coping with conflict that distracts us from following God's battle plan. It is our personal responsibility to use the Sword to capture our sinful thoughts, to defeat them, and to make our minds obey our Savior. Read the verses for yourself:

> *For though we walk in the flesh, we do not war*
> *after the flesh: (for the weapons of our warfare are*
> *not carnal, but mighty through God to the pulling*

down of strong holds;) casting down imagina-
tions, and every high thing that exalteth itself
against the knowledge of God, and bringing into
captivity every thought to the obedience of Christ.
(2 Corinthians 10:3–5)

TURNING POINT

The darkness within our flesh is scary. But as we face the darkness within, we remember anew God's amazing power over sin and how much He, the Creator of the entire universe, loves us.

How I wish I could tell you that Supermom never bothered to attack this soldier-mom again, but that would be a lie. She attacks me every day.

I *can* say that this battle for my mind was a defining moment for me. After this battle, I began to see my sinful nature as my enemy—a real enemy bent on destroying me. And that's when I named her Supermom. I asked God to help me see those attacks for what they were and to identify my battles as spiritual, rather than blaming my circumstances or the people around me. And He has helped me, because He loves me.

He loves you too, and He offers you as His child the same Sword of the Spirit for your *real* battles. Your Supermom won't offer it to you. Only He can. And only you can take it up and use it to wage war against your Supermom.

Even now as I write these words, Supermom is whispering in my ear. "Are you sure you want to tell total strangers all of this? Nobody really wants to hear your sob story. Be careful, Robin, you don't want to embarrass your husband or hurt his ministry, do you? Won't your parents be so disappointed to find out about your horrible thoughts? And what about your children? It seems unloving to involve them in this exposé of your own problems." And on she goes ever with me in this "body of death" (Romans 7:24).

And just now I waged war with her using this verse.

*Confess your faults one to another, and pray one
for another, that ye may be healed. (James 5:16)*

I've confessed to God, and I've confessed to you. Confession
of my sin directly to God is the most amazing, freeing experience. Because of Christ's covering over me and my sin, I have
direct access to God, Himself.

*Seeing then that we have a great high priest, that
is passed into the heavens, Jesus the Son of God,
let us hold fast our profession. . . . Let us therefore
come boldly unto the throne of grace, that we may
obtain mercy, and find grace to help in time of
need. (Hebrews 4:14, 16)*

Go to the throne of grace. You'll find true healing of your
spirit and mind there. Resting in Jesus is the answer for every
conflict because His Word alone holds the power to defeat your
sinful nature. And His Sword will defeat every single sin in our
heart. Every single one.

WHAT ABOUT ME?

1. My Supermom tempts me toward independence from
   God by overdependence on myself. Yours might do the
   same. Or maybe your Supermom takes the opposite
   approach with the same sin: independence from God
   by overdependence on others (spouse, friend, sister, or
   others). Which is your battlefield?

2. Can you pinpoint a period of time when you believe
   your mind was under spiritual attack? Frankly, most of
   our spiritual warfare begins in the mind, so you probably can think of several examples. Write them down.
   Write at least one example from the past and one battle
   you're fighting right now.

3. Then write down the false thoughts, questions, and
   beliefs that your Supermom used then and is using in
   each battle now to tempt you to doubt the love of your
   Father for you and to mistrust His character. Ask God

to give you wisdom to identify these and the courage to face them.

4. Now write down the verses you used or should have used to fight your Supermom in each battle. If you haven't already, memorize your battle verses. Take your time to sharpen your Sword. She will attack again. Be ready!

5. When you read the list of habits and spiritual activities that Supermom can use to distract us from dealing with the sin in our hearts (pages 24–25), did you see yourself on that list? Spend time considering your habits. While there is nothing inherently sinful about some of those habits, let the Holy Spirit lay your heart bare and consider whether your Supermom is distracting you and keeping you busy so you won't hear and heed His gentle promptings. Take the time to be painfully honest.

If I slip into the place that can be filled by
  Christ alone,
making myself the first necessity to a soul
instead of leading it to fasten upon Him,
then I know nothing of Calvary love.[1]

Amy Carmichael

Chapter Three
The Battle for Authority

HOW BAD IS SHE REALLY?

Do I really understand the horrible condition of my sinful nature? Of Supermom in me? I mean, how bad is she really? Am I being a bit dramatic here? Does she just have some selfish tendencies, or is she really rotten to the core? The Sword says,

> *The heart is deceitful above all things, and desperately wicked: who can know it? (Jeremiah 17:9)*

But wait a minute! The idea that we just need to trust our hearts has completely permeated our society and our thought processes. Are we saying then that our heart is *not* to be trusted? That Supermom *never* has our good in mind? That she will lead us to destruction every single time? Surely I have something good in me.

> *For the imagination of man's heart is evil from his youth. (Genesis 8:21)*

> *Also the heart of the sons of men is full of evil, and madness is in their heart while they live. (Ecclesiastes 9:3)*

For out of the heart proceed evil thoughts, murders, adulteries, fornications, thefts, false witness, blasphemies. (Matthew 15:19)

For from within, out of the heart of men, proceed evil thoughts, adulteries, fornications, murders, thefts, covetousness, wickedness, deceit, lasciviousness, an evil eye, blasphemy, pride, foolishness: All these evil things come from within, and defile the man. (Mark 7:21–23)

You might say, "I've always thought that if I just had enough confidence and faith in myself, things would eventually work out!"

It is better to trust in the Lord than to put confidence in man. (Psalm 118:8)

For I say, through the grace given unto me, to every man that is among you, not to think of himself more highly than he ought to think; but to think soberly, according as God hath dealt to every man the measure of faith. (Romans 12:3)

The Apostle Paul was no stranger to this battle you and I are fighting. He fought it every day. It's the age-old battle between our flesh and the Holy Spirit. Paul had every reason to have confidence in his own abilities, his own experience, his own super-evangelist. He had every single reason to be self-reliant in his generation.

Though I might also have confidence in the flesh. If any other man thinketh that he hath whereof he might trust in the flesh, I more: Circumcised the eighth day, of the stock of Israel, of the tribe of Benjamin, an Hebrew of the Hebrews; as touching the law, a Pharisee; Concerning zeal, persecuting the church; touching the righteousness which is in the law, blameless. (Philippians 3:4–6)

He goes on to explain that his natural abilities, his training, and his good actions, all things that he could have had confidence in, he considers worthless!

> *But what things were gain to me, those I counted*
> *loss for Christ. (Philippians 3:7)*

Read the following passage substituting "Supermom" (or "sinful nature") for the word "flesh" every time it occurs. It paints a vivid picture of just how serious the outcome of this battle really is.

> *Be not deceived; God is not mocked: for whatsoever*
> *a man soweth, that shall he also reap. For he that*
> *soweth to his flesh [Supermom] shall of the flesh*
> *[Supermom] reap corruption; but he that soweth*
> *to the Spirit shall of the Spirit reap life everlasting.*
> *(Galatians 6:7–8)*

And knowing in a very personal way that we'll get bone weary in this battle with Supermom, Paul adds, "And let us not be weary in well doing: for in due season we shall reap, if we faint not" (Galatians 6:9).

The battle is real! Paul, probably one of the most spiritual men ever to live, spells out our struggle plainly in Galatians 5:17. Read it carefully!

> *For the flesh [Supermom] lusteth against the Spirit,*
> *and the Spirit against the flesh [Supermom]: and*
> *these are contrary the one to the other: so that ye*
> *cannot do the things that ye would.*

He goes even deeper in describing his own personal battle with his flesh, in Romans 7. You can almost hear the frustration in his voice.

> *For that which I do I allow not: for what I would,*
> *that do I not; but what I hate, that do I. If then I*
> *do that which I would not, I consent unto the law*
> *that it is good. Now then it is no more I that do*
> *it, but sin that dwelleth in me. For I know that in*

> *me (that is, in my flesh,) dwelleth no good thing:*
> *for to will is present with me; but how to perform*
> *that which is good, I find not. For the good that*
> *I would I do not: but the evil which I would not,*
> *that I do. Now if I do that I would not, it is no*
> *more I that do it, but sin that dwelleth in me. . . .*
> *But I see another law in my members, warring*
> *against the law of my mind, and bringing me into*
> *captivity to the law of sin which is in my members.*
> *O wretched man that I am! who shall deliver me*
> *from the body of this death? (Romans 7:15–20,*
> *23–24)*

But then he considers the hope God has given us in Christ. He remembers that "There is therefore now no condemnation to them which are in Christ Jesus, who walk not after the flesh [Supermom], but after the Spirit. For the law of the Spirit of life in Christ Jesus hath made me free from the law of sin and death" (Romans 8:1–2).

And he gives us insight into the battle in our own hearts.

> *For they that are after the flesh [Supermom] do*
> *mind the things of the flesh [Supermom]; but they*
> *that are after the Spirit the things of the Spirit. For*
> *to be carnally minded is death; but to be spiritu-*
> *ally minded is life and peace. (Romans 8:5–6)*

Why does peace come only when we walk in the Spirit?

> *Because the carnal mind is enmity against God: for*
> *it is not subject to the law of God, neither indeed*
> *can be. So then they that are in the flesh cannot*
> *please God. (Romans 8:7–8)*

And he reminds us Christian soldier-moms that "ye are not in the flesh [Supermom], but in the Spirit, if so be that the Spirit of God dwell in you. . . . And if Christ be in you, the body is dead because of sin; but the Spirit is life because of righteousness" (Romans 8:9–10).

We have life because of Christ in us. That means we'll live eternally and will spend forever with Christ in heaven, but we also have something right here on earth that is powerful. We have the ability to defeat the sin in our hearts because of the Spirit He has given to us.

> *Therefore, brethren [sisters], we are debtors,*
> *not to the flesh [Supermom], to live after the*
> *flesh [Supermom]. For if ye live after the flesh*
> *[Supermom], ye shall die:* **but if ye through the**
> **Spirit do mortify the deeds of the body, ye**
> **shall live.** *(Romans 8:12–13)*

And that's it, sisters. We must every single day enter the battle against Supermom to put her to death! Sounds valiant, but what does it actually mean?

It's saying that because Christ has freed me from the power of sin eternally, I can choose to be free from sin's power today too. It's saying that if I live according to the dictates of Supermom, I'll surely destroy myself and others around me; but if I live through the power of the Holy Spirit and habitually put to death the evil deeds that she prompts me to do, not allowing them to have any power over me, I will live! We don't owe Supermom anything. She's our enemy.

This is the battle cry we must lift loud and long. Put her to death. Don't be deceived by her tactics anymore. Fight. *Never* give up.

Supermom is bad. She's evil. And she's bent on destroying us. She's determined to destroy my children too and delights in using me to do it!

As a Christian, I know she can't have my spirit. My spirit belongs to my Father and will live eternally with Him in heaven. But she does still have the ability to tempt me, harass me, and battle me for authority over my soul—my will, my mind, my emotions. I have a target on my back. She hates me. She hates that I'm created in God's image. She's angry that God has rescued my spirit from her evil. And she'll do everything in her power to destroy me in the attempt to get back at my God for loving me. She's that wicked.

She wants authority. She lusts for power and she wants me to love the power authority brings too. She comes to me deceitfully, and she skillfully uses my role as a mother to whet my appetite for power and authority over my children.

PLAYING GOD

When my children were preschoolers, I decided it was time to start teaching them about good character qualities like responsibility, kindness, joyfulness, diligence. The teacher in me came out in full force. I printed up each character trait on a colorful card with its definition and a coordinating Bible verse. I'd sit them in a circle, and we'd memorize the definitions and verses together and talk about ways they could make good choices that day—like being kind to their sister, putting their toys away with a cheerful spirit, and always, always being diligent to flush the toilet rather than saving it for a show-and-tell session.

I'll never forget the day I introduced the concept of *initiative* to them. They listened obediently and repeated the definition back to me in their sweet sing-songy voices: "*Initiative* is seeing what needs to be done and doing it without having to be asked." Two of them even offered ways they could show initiative—putting on their seat belts before being told or not using the neon blue toothpaste as an art medium on the bathroom cabinet. I was grateful for their insights.

But then one son who had sat quietly contemplating his siblings' ideas asked me an innocent and perceptive question that made me stop in my know-it-all teacher tracks: "But Mommy, how can we ever show initiative if you're always telling us what to do?"

How could they indeed? Here I was asking them to have the foresight to see what they should do and then do it without being asked. The problem was, I was so accustomed to directing those little bodies and controlling their every move that I never even gave them the opportunity to do so for themselves.

Obviously preschoolers need direction. I'm not advocating a freestyle parenting approach here. But what is our ultimate goal? You should write your own goals out, but mine include raising children who love God with all their hearts and are responsible adults. For them to become responsible, I must allow them to take small baby steps in character growth along the way, but not just get them to conform to my expectations.

I was convicted of my controlling habits over my children. I also became a bit fearful as I considered what future conversations with this son in his teenage years might be like. He had beaten me already and he was only four. *Sigh*.

Was I really that controlling? Did I really think that their future happiness and safety depended upon my ability to control their environment, to manipulate their circumstances, to teach them how to succeed in this world, and to direct their every single move to my satisfaction?

Did I really think that highly of myself? I had a problem. A problem so obvious that even my four year old could see it.

The battle was on. Supermom wanted me and my children to think that I had absolute power over them. God's Spirit says that God alone has that authority.

Supermom wanted me to "play God."

GOD'S ALONE

Studying God's attributes helped me defeat Supermom's thirst for authority in my children's lives. Depending on the theologian you study, there are several methods of dividing up God's attributes and even variations of their actual definitions.

But among the most familiar of God's attributes obvious to us laywomen are *omnipresence*, *omnipotence*, and *omniscience*. These attributes are inseparable from the very being of God and are a permanent part of who He is. In fact, they *are* who He is.

Supermom hates God. She wants to take the place of God in my heart. She wants *me* to take the place of God in my children's hearts too. Supermom actually tries on a very regular basis to get me to display the attributes that are inherent only to God.

Ms. Controlling

She tempts me to try my hand at being omnipresent with my children. Webster defines *omnipresence* as being *present everywhere simultaneously.* Attempting to keep an eye on three wiggling bodies going in three different directions is a challenge, but she loves to nag me with guilt if I don't at least try to be a "good mom." She secretly laughs while she watches me run myself ragged, rather than take reasonable precautions with my children but trust their overall safety to their Creator.

She wants me to live in fear for their safety. She wants me to knock myself out by trying to control every circumstance, every germ, every person, every influence, every moment of my child's day and night. She wants to rob me of the joy of experiencing life through their eyes by teaching them to live in fear of what *might happen.* And by keeping me stressed out trying to control their lives, she wants me to demonstrate daily for them that God's love isn't trustworthy. She doesn't want me to trust in God. She doesn't want my children to see me trusting in God.

I remember the most life-altering wake-up call that my children's lives are in the hands of their loving Creator—and not mine. It was December. I was eight months pregnant with the twins, and Cotter was fifteen months old. I had been condemned to bed rest. My own dear mother and precious mother-in-law had been taking turns flying up to the north woods to take care of Cotter and me while I carried out my sentence.

My mom-in-law had just left after two weeks of taking care of my family, and in two days my own mom would arrive for her shift. But for now I was on my own. It was Christmas break, and almost everyone in our university neighborhood had cleared out for warmer regions. Even our neighbors were gone for Christmas travels.

Bobby had driven a student down to the airport in Green Bay an hour and a half away. I had been assigned to just stay home and rest with Cotter. But I didn't listen. I was restless. I was tired of being locked up in my house. I wanted *out*. And I was sure I could handle a quick run to the dumpster to take a few bags of trash. Anything to get out of the house. Obviously I was desperate if trash dumping sounded appealing. Any of you who have ever served time in bed rest know exactly what I'm talking about.

I waddled out to the garage and loaded the van with the trash. Then I started the van to warm it up by blasting the heater. (Don't worry, the garage door was open.)

I carefully bundled Cotter up in his snowsuit, hat, gloves, and boots. I honestly don't know what I was thinking. He wasn't going to feel the cold air since he wasn't even going to leave his car seat.

I didn't dress myself so carefully. Since I was just going to toss a few garbage bags into the dumpster, I wore some flimsy shoes, my light leather jacket, and no gloves. So dumb.

Anyway, I carefully buckled him in and put my purse with cell phone on the front seat of the van. Then I went back and responsibly locked the house up. That was when I realized I had locked my keys and cell phone in the car . . . with it running . . . and myself out of the house.

And there was my sweet little baby smiling at me through the van window.

I felt the first bit of alarm sweep through me. Bobby was gone. My closest neighbors were gone. Even if I broke into my house, I couldn't call Bobby since my cell phone was in the car, and we couldn't make long-distance phone calls on our home phone.

I shuffled out to the ice- and snow-covered driveway, calculating how long it would take me to walk to the nearest house where somebody might be home. In my condition, too long. We live spaced far apart from our neighbors in the woods, and I couldn't leave my son!

I dragged myself back to the car, smiling and doing funny faces to Cotter through the window, begging God not to let him see my tears or rising terror. No need for him to be scared too.

I decided I had to break into the house and call for local help. So I slipped and skated my giant pregnant body down the hill to the basement apartment on back of our house, grabbed the metal snow shovel, and tried to break the window of the back door. Over and over and over. It wouldn't budge. What window glass doesn't break under the force of a crazed, crying, pregnant woman slinging a weapon at it? Tempered glass, that's what.

On my way up the icy hill back to the driveway, I had my first contraction. Real panic set in. I mentally pictured myself giving birth to twins in the snow by myself with Cotter watching from the van.

I checked on Cotter again, smiling and waving like everything was fine and we were just playing some sort of game together. His little face was bright red and little beads of sweat were running down his cheeks. He smiled at me patiently and waved. Precious baby. He'd been in there for a good thirty minutes by now.

Another contraction hit.

The only other way into the house was through one of the front windows, I reasoned. They were set pretty high up on the house for an eight-month-pregnant girl. But nothing stops a mother bear when her cub is in danger. Not frozen feet. Not frozen hands. Not contractions. Not windows.

I grabbed a large plastic bin, dragged it under one of our front windows, teetered precariously on it, and, remembering my complete failure at the back window, drove the corner of the metal snow shovel at it with all my strength. No tempered glass in the front. It shattered into a bazillion pieces all over our living room.

Another contraction.

I hauled my body through that front window with its hanging shards of glass and called a friend for help. God alone helped this girl through that window uncut.

Within five minutes several friends were there. Cotter was rescued. I was put back to bed. Bobby was called. The glass was cleaned up. The window was boarded. They even took the trash to the dumpster for me. And I didn't give birth to the twins that day.

I felt so loved by these friends who came to my rescue. But I also felt like a fool for getting myself in this mess in the first place. God, knowing my tendency to be self-sufficient, let me experience my inadequacy firsthand. I wasn't omnipresent. He is.

Ms. Know-it-All

Supermom isn't finished. She whispers that I must also be omniscient. Webster defines this quality as *having total knowledge or knowing everything*. I quickly discovered that attempting to answer all my children's little questions while acting as if I know everything can wear me down. I find that I sometimes cut them short with impatience or just make up an answer to get them off my back. She justifies my lack of love toward my children by offering me the quick rationalization that they are, after all, just nagging children and that no one is capable of being *that* patient. I've also been tempted to just make up answers for them if I don't know the answer, modeling for them how to master the ability of white lies. Sometimes I'm completely at a loss for words when confronted by my preschooler's questions, questions like, "Mommy, if all the gravity cells in our body die at the same time, would we float to the moon?" Supermom loves when I give in to the art of deception at any level. She is, after all, quite a fan of lying.

She enjoys playing up to my fear of looking like a fool in front of anyone (even curious toddlers) and is satisfied when my fear of man trumps my fear of God.

She loves for me to be impatient and irritable at their pestering, giving them the clear impression that their questions are unworthy to be answered, that somehow I'm better than they are, and that they are an irritant to me.

She loves it when I forget my own petty prayers to my loving Father. She wants me to forget how patient He is, and how He welcomes even His straying children with loving open arms, and never, never turns me away when I need to come speak with Him in the name of His Son.

She wants my children to value their own reasoning abilities above God's. She wants me to teach them by my daily example how to arrogantly turn up their noses at those whose intellectual abilities don't equal their own.

Ms. In-Charge

Supermom also wants me to be omnipotent, or as Webster defines it, I should have *unlimited or universal power and authority.* God created the role of *Mom* to be the great healer of ouches and scrapes and little wounded spirits, the fixer-upper of broken toys, and the one who discerns the motives of a child's heart and gives hands down judgment on wrong actions. She even has the power to both determine and carry out punishments. Supermom urges me to make the most of this power and to enjoy all the perks that come with such absolute authority over my children. In other words, if they don't do what I want them to, I can make them pay for it. If they get in the way of my agenda, they'll regret it.

Supermom loves to see my children cringe in fear before me rather than cheerfully obey. She loves when my children put me on a pedestal in their little hearts, because she relishes the excitement of the day she will watch me fall and my children flounder in disillusionment and resentment because they find out who I really am—a selfish, power-hungry, fearful sinner.

MOTIVATED BY FEAR

Did you see the common thread of my attempts to play God? Unchecked, ungodly fear was the motive behind each of them. I want to control my children's actions because I'm afraid something might happen to them. I want to have all the answers because I don't want them to trust anyone else the way they trust me. And I'm not above using fear to control their behavior if that's what it takes to maintain my position of authority in their little lives. Wow. Fear.

Supermom used fear to motivate me. She's so clever. Once again, she had perverted a good thing—my role as a protector, teacher, and discipler of my children—by twisting it into something that brought me control, satisfaction, and power.

Let's take the most un-Christlike example there is in the Bible of this sin and go all the way back to Lucifer. We read about him in Isaiah 14:12–14.

> *How art thou fallen from heaven, O Lucifer, son of the morning! How art thou cut down to the ground, which didst weaken the nations! For thou hast said in thine heart, **I will** ascend into heaven, **I will** exalt my throne above the stars of God: **I will** sit also upon the mount of the congregation, in the sides of the north: **I will** ascend above the heights of the clouds; **I will** be like the most High.*

He wanted to be *like God*. Take note of how many times he says "I will." He obviously had convinced himself that becoming God was really a possibility!

And yet, here is Supermom, a very intimate part of our hearts. She is convinced of her capabilities and confident of her success. Just like Lucifer.

I am certain that our loving, sovereign God daily orchestrates the events surrounding our home and children to create opportunities for us to see our sin, acknowledge our dependence on Him, and then experience His overwhelming love.

His gifts to us often include reminders of our *place*, our role in our children's lives. God began to teach me that my chief goal is not to *be* God to my children. My goal is to be the primary channel that points them *to* God. They need to see my weakness. Okay, we all agree that part's not so hard. They live with us 24/7, so they can't help but see our weakness. In fact, the ones at home see us at our weakest points more than anyone else ever will.

But that's only part of it. Now comes the challenge. They need to see me take my weakness to the throne of grace and acknowledge it to God. They need to see me depend on God for wisdom, for physical strength, for health, for provision, for unconditional love, and for the very endurance required to clean up after children day after day. They need to see me confront my sin of playing God in their lives and deal with it. They need to see how to defeat this sin in their own lives.

THE BATTLE

It is time to pick up my Sword and do battle with Supermom. Supermom wants my children to wrongly think I can see everything they are doing and live in fear of me. But the Sword says I should be teaching my children that "the eyes of the Lord run to and fro throughout the whole earth, to shew himself strong in the behalf of them whose heart is perfect toward him" (2 Chronicles 16:9).

My children need to know that their mom can't see or control everything they're doing, but their God can see them, and that He wants to bless them when they do right. He is their ultimate protector. Not me.

> *The Lord is thy keeper: the Lord is thy shade upon thy right hand. The sun shall not smite thee by day, nor the moon by night. The Lord shall preserve thee from all evil: he shall preserve thy soul. The Lord shall preserve thy going out and thy coming in from this time forth, and even for evermore. (Psalm 121:5–8)*

> *The name of the Lord is a strong tower: the righteous runneth into it, and is safe. (Proverbs 18:10)*

Supermom wants my children to think I have all the answers. She wants to set me up on a pedestal in their eyes so that they think more highly of me than they should. She wants all their praise and respect. She selfishly wants my children to need me more than God to meet the desire in my heart for affirmation that *should* only come from God.

But the Sword says God is the source of all wisdom, not me.

> *If any of you lack wisdom, let him ask of God, that giveth to all men liberally . . . and it shall be given him. (James 1:5)*

The Sword says that if they want wisdom, they must fear God not their mom.

> *The fear of the Lord is the beginning of wisdom. (Proverbs 9:10)*

Supermom wants them to believe I hold ultimate authority over them and have the power to make things happen for them, but the Sword says God holds the ultimate authority over our lives and that He sees not only what we do, but why we do it.

> *The horse is prepared against the day of battle: but safety is of the Lord. (Proverbs 21:31)*

> *Every way of a man is right in his own eyes: but the Lord pondereth the hearts. (Proverbs 21:2)*

These children are not mine. They belong to God. They are His creation. I am simply a steward of the time I have with them. I have been given a holy charge to train them, meet their physical needs, and demonstrate God's love daily by loving them. My greatest joy is the thought that when I look at them, I'm looking at potential brothers and sisters in Christ with whom I will spend eternity. And God has given me the privilege of a few years here on earth to point them to Him.

When my children do look to me, I want them to know that I will petition God's throne for them on their behalf and that I will teach them they can gain access to our Father's throne of grace through the blood of their Savior.

I want them to know that God sees everything and holds me and them personally accountable for our actions and thoughts.

I want them to know that God's Word pierces even to the motives of our hearts, that He has all wisdom and gives it liberally to those who ask for it, and that He holds all power and protects and defends His children.

They need to know that I am not Supermom. They need to see how to live a life dependent on God for its very breath. They need to see living humility in my spirit.

> And [God] said unto me, My grace is sufficient for
> thee: for my strength is made perfect in weakness.
> (2 Corinthians 12:9)

When I am Supermom, they stand in awe of me. But in my weakness, they will stand in awe of God.

WHAT ABOUT ME?

1. Have you ever stopped to consider just how bad your Supermom is? Re-read the verses about the depth of depravity in our human hearts. It's not talking about depraved humankind in general; those verses are talking about you, about me, about *our* hearts. Let the Holy Spirit use His Word to root out any self-reliance, self-confidence, or self-praise you find lingering in your heart.

2. My Supermom tempts me to try to *be* God to my children—to take His place in their hearts. It may be that your Supermom tempts you in a different approach, perhaps leading you to be so laissez faire in your parenting style that your children know nothing of the necessity of obedience or the protection of a loving parent who sets wise boundaries and gives consequences for disobedience. This parenting style teaches children to take the throne in their own lives, rather than submitting to God's authority. Either extreme accomplishes Supermom's goals: a child so dependent on himself or others that he has no need for God in his life. When your Supermom tempts you to err in your parenting style, toward which extreme do you tend?

3. In what ways have you been motivated by fear in your

life and in your parenting? Consider whether your Supermom has tempted you to be too controlling, too arrogantly knowledgeable, or too powerful to your children, usurping the place that belongs only to God in their hearts.

4. Consider the parenting style under which you were reared. Were your parents too strict or too permissive? How has their parenting style influenced how you are rearing your children?

5. When your children leave your home as adults, how do you want to be remembered? Think it through. Pray about it. Write it down. Compare your goals to the Bible. Can you fully support your parenting goals in Scripture? If not, revise your goals based on Scripture.

I would be humble,
For I know my weakness.[1]

Howard A. Walter

Chapter Four

The Battle of Pride

I'm that woman.

I'm that woman thrown at the feet of Jesus in bondage to my sin, deserving of punishment and complete condemnation.

I'm that woman the Pharisees disgustedly, proudly set publicly before Jesus for His judgment.

I'm that woman in need of mercy, but not daring to ask for it and in full knowledge of my guilt, my sin, and the depth of blackness within my own heart.

All my life I felt sorry for this woman at the feet of Jesus. Her horrible, public sin. Caught. Guilty. At the mercy of the law. She was truly a sinful woman. A woman who didn't deserve anything from Jesus.

I always took some comfort in the fact that I haven't done what she did. I haven't ever made such a public habit of sin, haven't ever stained my reputation that way, haven't ever defiled my body that way. I was just on a different plane than she was, by God's grace, of course, but still somehow better than she.

How dare I? How dare I stand aloof as an unattached observer of this scene unfolded in God's Word? As a bystander watching her meet her fate? If I only stand by and judge, I'm one of the Pharisees in this scene. If I only stand by and judge, I can't receive the mercy of Jesus.

Like she did.

If I'm not she in this moment, then I won't hear Jesus strip away everything but Himself as He reveals the hearts of others who condemn me.

> *He that is without sin among you, let him first cast*
> *a stone at her. (John 8:7)*

I won't hear the sound of my critics slinking away in the face of His truth in their sudden understanding of their own sin.

> *And they which heard it, being convicted by their*
> *own conscience, went out one by one, beginning at*
> *the eldest, even unto the last. (John 8:9)*

I won't hear Jesus ask me that question that He asks her to show me He alone has the power to judge her or to judge me for sin.

> *Woman, where are those thine accusers? (John 8:10)*

I won't understand in the blinding flash of that moment that I'm fully at the mercy of my Savior, like she did.

And then I will miss the most precious moment of all, that moment when Jesus spoke to her guilty heart those powerful words of forgiveness, of amazing love, of comfort, of direction.

> *Neither do I condemn thee: go, and sin no more.*
> *(John 8:11)*

Forgiveness. Mercy undeserved, full and complete by the only One able to condemn me.

Her sin had been revealed. She had been publicly humiliated, and she must have been overwhelmed by His forgiveness. Her life had just been saved. She had just encountered her Creator. And she had been truly loved.

I hadn't really done horrible things. I was known as a "good girl." Supermom had compiled a lengthy and satisfying mental list of those I personally knew who had sinned bigger than I had. Poor souls.

But I did feel a strange sense of loss. I thought somehow that since I had avoided big sins, the publicly condemned sins, I might never really understand Jesus' comments to Simon about the sinful woman who couldn't stop worshipping Him, weeping over Him, and loving Him.

> Her sins, which are many, are forgiven; for she loved much: but to whom little is forgiven, the same loveth little. (Luke 7:47)

Oh, what a precious day when Jesus showed me that I am that woman, every bit as sinful and every bit in need of forgiveness as she was.

If I never understand the depth of sin in my own heart, I'll never begin to grasp the depth of His mercy, of His sacrifice, and of His love for me. I will love Him too little.

Yes, I am that woman. Guilty.

Sinner, like she is, because of who I am.

Forgiven, like she is, because of Who He is.

Loved, like she is, because He chose to.

One day in heaven, I'll meet her, this woman so much like myself, forgiven and loved by Jesus. And together, we'll praise Him forever.

THE SIN

But just how I had I gotten to this place in line next to the Pharisees? I was comfortable there evidently. I had been an observer of this woman for years, a watcher and a detached judge, just like them.

How is it that I didn't see my sin for what it was? Was I really that blind? Had I really been *(gulp)* deceived just like Eve had been? What had blinded me? What tool of Supermom had she been using on me all these years? It was obviously a good one! And suddenly I knew.

Pride.

I was full of pride, just like Lucifer is and just like the Pharisees were.

But being the clever diva she is, Supermom had colored my ugly pride beautiful new colors—colors that hid its true identity from my own eyes. Remember that she represents my sinful nature, which aligns her with Lucifer, the one who comes as the "angel of light" (2 Corinthians 11:14). So when I did consider these areas of my life, I didn't see my true motives and was willing to call these issues something else more palatable to my spiritual tastes:

- like *my rights*. Every mom just needs to take time for herself, for heaven's sake.

- like *my impatience* with my children, with my husband. Why did they treat me as if I was their slave? They didn't even appreciate me. And why couldn't they just see things my way? I'm not being unreasonable to expect them to carry their plates to the sink after I've fixed them their dinner.

- like *my strong personality*. That's just who I am, and God made me, of course. Everyone else could just deal with it.

- like *the fact that I didn't view myself as an emotionally "needy" person*, praise the Lord. Those poor girls who have to be surrounded by others constantly to get their needs for security met always had my sympathy.

Wow. I was full of pride.

And God in His perfect love wasn't willing that I should stay deceived. His Word is so very powerful and able to lay our hearts open—even to us.

WEAPON OF POWER

Have you ever really considered just how powerful our Sword, the Word of God, is? We've talked about this verse before, but let's consider it again.

> *For the word of God is quick, and powerful, and sharper than any twoedged sword, piercing even*

*to the dividing asunder of soul and spirit, and of
the joints and marrow, and is a discerner of the
thoughts and intents of the heart. (Hebrews 4:12)*

God's Word is quick. It's alive. It's energizing. It gives life!

God's Word is powerful. It's strong and effective. It convinces persuasively; it convicts deeply; it comforts fully.

It's sharper than a two-edged sword. It cuts both ways, clean and precise, revealing what is there.

It divides my soul and spirit, laying my will, my emotions, and my mind open and exposed.

It discerns my thoughts, every single hidden, cringing, selfish, secret, sinful thought I've ever considered. But that is not deep enough yet.

It goes all the way down to the very motive of my heart, the reasons I do every single thing I do and then it lays them open for me to see.

Wow. That's the amazing Word, and it's amazing because of its author, God Himself.

Not only is it my Sword with the power to defeat Supermom fully, but also it can be turned in upon my own heart for the purpose of giving me life and for the purpose of showing me who I really am so I can fight those battles and be free of sin's domination in this body, in this life. Amazing.

The problem, of course, is that when the Word of God cuts us open and we see ourselves for who we really are, we are faced with a very clear question. What am I going to do about what is revealed? And that was the question I had to answer. I wanted to walk away and pretend I wasn't under conviction. I wanted to ignore it. Supermom circled close by, intently watching me, waiting to see what I'd do.

When I decided I must deal with my pride in the light of God's Word, Supermom moved in for the attack. She wasn't about to go down without a kicking, screaming fight. Pride is a precious gem in her crown.

A MOM'S RIGHT TO HER RIGHTS

Take my rights, for example. Everyone says that as a woman, I have rights. Supermom certainly agrees with society's general consensus on the subject. Since I'm an American, even my nation's constitution says that my rights are God-given, not government-granted. And I'm forever grateful for that.

Webster defines a *right* as something that *justly belongs to one.* It's *a fair claim to something, a privilege by birth or creed.*

Supermom has cleverly appealed to our natural sense of self-worth and has convinced us women that we have certain unalienable rights because of our sex, because of our role. That people owe us. And more specifically, she has carefully taught us that we are fully justified in defending our rights.

My list of rights was long, and it sounded quite reasonable to me. Supermom had also given her stamp of approval, and so we had never quarreled about them. I had

- the right to a full night's sleep now and then;

- the right to a husband who loves me;

- the right to children who are obedient;

- the right to protect me-time;

- the right to a clean house;

- the right to be praised for what I do;

- the right to be appreciated by my family; and

- the right to have my needs met.

Up to this point, I'm not even sure I had really admitted to myself that I was resentfully holding on to these rights.

I hadn't actually clearly communicated my rights to my family members, but I had certainly implied them. And every time they violated one of my rights, I let them know through the vehicle of my impatience and anger. I felt fully justified in doing so.

I actually had never realized that I had an anger problem. I'm serious. I always thought of myself as a calm, even-mannered person capable of keeping her cool and her sense of humor even when teaching a history class of junior high students every day. In fact, I was so full of pride about my lack of anger that God decided to put me in just the right circumstances to show me what was really in my heart and to show me what He already knew was there.

He gave me three toddlers.

I had been prideful about my right *actions* under pressure, but it was my sinful *reactions* that revealed who I really was. Reactions are spontaneous and unplanned. I can carefully calculate my actions, but I can't truly react with anything that's not already in me.

It's like a hot cup of coffee. When the coffee cup is bumped, coffee spills over. When I'm bumped, what's in my heart will spill over too, and those around me will experience firsthand the contents of my cup.

And when I spilled over, it wasn't pretty. Sometimes it was seething frustration. Sometimes it was explosive. Sometimes it was cold silence. Sometimes it was in guilt-inflicting words. Always it was unloving.

I used my anger to threaten my children into obedience, to show them how disappointed I was in them, to belittle them, to punish them, to make them feel like my love for them was conditional on their behavior, to model for them everything that God's love is not.

What unreasonable expectations I had of my toddlers. How could they possibly have acted any other way? Of course they were disobedient and selfish. They had no choice. They were born sinners, and they didn't have the Spirit of God to help them defeat their own sinful natures yet. In fact, we their parents are the ones who gave them their sin natures. And now I'm berating them for having one?

They didn't need me to judge them for who they were. They needed me to love them, just like God loved me when I was a sinner.

> *But God commendeth His love toward us, in*
> *that, while we were yet sinners, Christ died for us.*
> *(Romans 5:8)*

And here I was, their *Christian* mom with the Spirit of God living inside of me ready to help me defeat Supermom, and I was acting just like they were in selfish arrogance because I wasn't getting what I wanted—their cooperative, good behavior. I had the power to defeat sin, and I was choosing instead to live in defeat.

What a great mom I had turned out to be. *Sigh.*

After my anger flared and died down, I'd feel guilty—guilty for losing my temper, guilty for yelling at my children, guilty for acting like a toddler, and guilty for failing in self-control once again. And Supermom soothed my guilt-ridden conscience by reminding me that it really wasn't my fault. It was those sinful children God gave me. They made me mad. They caused me to get angry.

But the truth was that it wasn't their fault. Their disobedience just jostled my cup of selfishness so that my selfishness splashed out for all to see. I shudder to think of how many onlookers in Walmart never saw Jesus in the way I spoke to my children there.

EXCUSES VERSUS CONFESSION

Supermom stepped right up, put her arm around me, and sympathetically offered me the very convenient blame game, just as the devil offered it to Adam in Genesis 3:9–12 when Adam was trying to explain to God why he had sinned in the garden of Eden. Adam tells God in verse 12 that "the woman whom thou gavest to be with me, she gave me of the tree, and I did eat."

As it turns out, Supermom's tricks on us aren't that new after all. She ultimately wants me to take my grief out on God and blame Him for what He's given to me. He's the one that gave me those toddlers.

God was using my children to reveal what was in my heart so that I could deal with it, but Supermom wanted me to run from what was in my heart and blame my children and God for my conviction. I was under conviction, and I didn't like it.

Remember the main difference between Saul and David? They were both chosen and anointed by God, both successful military leaders, both physically attractive. But Saul ended up committing suicide, while David is known as a man "after God's own heart."

Neither was perfect. Saul disobeyed God by not following God's direct command to destroy his enemies. David disobeyed God by lusting after and sleeping with another man's wife and then having her husband killed. Significant sins for sure.

But the difference was their individual response to conviction. When Samuel confronted Saul for his disobedience, there is no record of any humility, any acknowledgement of his sin, any admission of wrongdoing. In fact, Saul offers a very spiritual-sounding explanation for his actions in 1 Samuel 15:15. He wanted to use the animals he allowed to live as sacrifices to God. He had what he thought was a very legitimate reason for his disobedience.

When Nathan confronted David with his sin of lust, adultery, and murder, David immediately and completely broke. His first response was, "I have sinned against the Lord" (2 Samuel 12:13).

And now it was my turn. I was under conviction for my sin of anger. Would I blame someone else? Would I make excuses for it? Would I offer God and others a spiritual sounding explanation for my sin like Saul did? Or would I acknowledge my sin, humble myself, and confess it to God?

Wait a minute. I was trying to deal with my pride here! Why was God confronting me with my sin of anger? Because depending on the individual and the circumstances, pride has the amazing chameleon-like ability to cloak itself in other manifestations. For some it's deceit; for others it's manipulation; for me it was anger. Pride's sinful manifestations, effects on others, and consequences are no less painful or far-reaching than the sin of pride itself and so must be confronted by the Sword.

I'm reminded of the time I watched a few lumberjacks cut down some giant old trees that were threatening our house. They didn't just go in and immediately chop the trees down. They carefully considered the largest limbs that hovered over our house and skillfully removed them first so as not to cause any damage. Then they went for the trunk. Similarly, in dealing with the rooted tree of pride in our lives, it may be necessary to first deal with some of its limbs and the effects those limbs have had on those around us.

Yes, it may be quickest to just yank out the tree by the root, and sometimes that's the best way. Remember the verses about cutting off your hand if it causes you to sin? (See Mark 9:43.) There is definitely a time for radical amputation.

But sometimes that radical amputation happens best one limb at a time. Eventually the tree is completely destroyed, but we've also been forced to deal with the pain we've caused to others in the various manifestations of our primary sin. In my case, pride manifested itself in anger.

The battle lines were drawn.

THE BATTLE

The Sword reminded me that "God resisteth the proud, but giveth grace unto the humble. Submit yourselves therefore to God. Resist the devil, and he will flee from you. Draw nigh to God, and he will draw nigh to you. Cleanse your hands, ye sinners; and purify your hearts, ye double minded. Be afflicted, and mourn, and weep: let your laughter be turned to mourning, and your joy to heaviness. Humble yourselves in the sight of the Lord, and he shall lift you up" (James 4:6b–10).

Confession and sorrow for my anger. Sorrow. This was the first time in a long time, I admit, that I actually felt real gut-wrenching grief and sorrow for my sin against God, against my children. When was the last time I felt sorrow over my sin?

When was the last time you did? Not regret or a disappointment for our failings, but real painful heartache over our sin?

God forgave me then just like He'll forgive you. Humility and confession is all it takes. I took David's route, not Saul's. You can too.

Confession of my sin was the turning point of my battle, but it certainly wasn't over yet. I still had to deal with my habit of anger.

The Sword said, "Robin, 'The wrath of man worketh not the righteousness of God' " (James 1:20).

Supermom countered, "But your children deserve your anger. They were disobedient and need to know that their disobedience has consequences. A loving mom teaches her children this rule."

And God said, "Dearly beloved, avenge not yourselves, but rather give place unto wrath: for it is written, Vengeance is mine; I will repay, saith the Lord" (Romans 12:19).

"Okay," I argued, "I'm not supposed be God to them, but I'm their mom. They need to see my anger so that they'll do right next time."

But God said, "Fathers [Mothers] provoke not your children to anger, lest they be discouraged" (Colossians 3:21).

"Okay," I conceded, "my anger only discouraged them. It didn't motivate them to obey next time."

Supermom wouldn't give up, of course. "You're supposed to be like Jesus," she exclaimed, "and He hates sin!"

But she clearly didn't know why Jesus had come to this earth in the first place. Jesus said in John 12:47 that He didn't come to judge the world. He came to save it. And I'm supposed to be like Jesus and let His mind be in me having compassion on people and loving them unconditionally. That includes loving my children.

Quickly Supermom changed her tactic. She appealed to my sense of control by flattering me.

"Okay," she agreed, "just work harder on not getting angry all the time. It's not becoming of you anyway. You need to be more patient. Try harder to be patient." And then she even used a verse on me!

> *Be not hasty in thy spirit to be angry: for anger*
> *resteth in the bosom of fools. (Ecclesiastes 7:9)*

Do you see what she did? She's so good at deceiving me! She encouraged me to do something right—to be patient—but she encouraged me to make it happen in my own strength. She wants the credit for any success I have in controlling my temper. She certainly doesn't want me to acknowledge that nothing good is in her, my flesh. That there was absolutely no way I could control my temper without the Spirit of God radically changing me.

The Sword reminded me *again*, "For I know that in me (that is, in my flesh,) dwelleth no good thing: for to will is present with me; but how to perform that which is good I find not" (Romans 7:18).

In other words, I might have the desire to do something good—like control my temper—but I don't have the power within me to do it. I don't have the ability to control it no matter how hard I try.

With smirky sneakiness, Supermom was setting me up for failure again. She wanted me to try to do "that which is good" in my own strength so that I'd crash and burn and start the guilt cycle all over again. This was becoming a pattern in my life it seemed. It was in this battle over my deep-rooted pride that I finally saw that cycle for that it was—a clever scheme of Supermom. My flesh was bent on destroying me and hurting my children in the process.

"Okay, so I can't control my temper in my flesh. Then how can I change? How can I find victory over my temper?"

And the Sword reminded me that God was the source of my victory.

> *What shall we then say to these things? If God be*
> *for us, who can be against us? He that spared not*
> *his own Son, but delivered him up for us all, how*
> *shall he not with him also freely give us all things?*
> *(Romans 8:31–32)*

And then the Sword repeated to me once again the absolute foolproof plan of action to defeat Supermom. It's your plan too, sister. Read it slowly. Jesus says, "Abide in me, and I in you. As the branch cannot bear fruit of itself, except it abide in the vine; no more can ye, **except ye abide in me**. I am the vine, ye are the branches: He that abideth in me, and I in him, the same bringeth forth much fruit: **for without me ye can do nothing**. . . . If ye abide in me, and my words abide in you, ye shall ask what ye will, and it shall be done unto you. Herein is my Father glorified, that ye bear much fruit; so shall ye be my disciples. As the Father hath loved me, so have I loved you: continue ye in my love (John 15:4–5, 7–9).

The emphasis here is not that we bear fruit. It's not that we just work harder to be patient, or to be kind, or to be content. It's that we *abide* in Jesus, our Savior. He knows we can't win by ourselves, and He loves us so much that He'll take care of the Supermom in our hearts for us if we just abide in Him. Just abide. He doesn't want me to produce any fruit. That's His job. He wants me to rest in Him.

Have you ever heard a branch grunting and groaning out loud in its attempt to grow fruit, straining to put that apple out there for all to see? Of course not! A branch is connected to the tree trunk where it just rests, where it just abides. The trunk and root system sends the branch everything it needs to be alive. And the fruit is a natural result of what's already happening inside the trunk.

Just abide. Just stay connected so closely to Jesus that His presence overflows out of your life.

But how do I actually do that? What does *abide* look like in my house? In my schedule? In my world? The time and place can be completely flexible. The point is that it happens, that every single day we take time to spend targeted time with our God, and that throughout the day—with every single breath—we walk in His Spirit.

I abide when:

- I'm doing the dishes.

- I'm potty-training my child.

- I'm talking on the phone.

- I'm scrubbing the toilet.

- I'm working.

- I'm arbitrating between my children.

I confess to you that this seemed hard to me at first. It wasn't my habit to be so dependent on God's Spirit. Supermom had me hoodwinked into thinking that I could pretty much handle life on my own.

But I can tell you that abiding in Jesus *works*. It gives you victory over Supermom, and it keeps us from being dependent on ourselves. It breaks the guilt cycle.

But far more than just getting victory, abiding in Jesus is an amazingly personal encounter with your Savior. Abiding in Him allows us to experience His love like never before. In fact the more we abide in Him, the more we want to, the more we can't imagine *not* abiding in Him, and the more desperate we are to rest in Him alone.

BACK TO MY RIGHTS

As I began to really abide in Jesus, He took me back to the issue that had gotten me into trouble in the first place—my rights.

One of Supermom's strongest attacks comes riding in on my rights and what I think I deserve. Her cheerleaders from the woman's liberation movement scream their support from the sidelines.

Do I really deserve to be publicly humiliated on a regular basis by my children? I know that happens to you too.

I remember the time I kept three-year old Cotter in the morning church service with me since he had a runny nose. (You know the other moms don't appreciate it much when you bring your sick kid into the nursery for him to share his germs with his peers.) I decided that morning to avoid the frustrated glances of other moms and keep my kiddo with me in the service. It was the last time I did it that year.

As the offering plate was about to be passed, I gave Cotter a quarter to put into the plate. I whispered that this money was for us to give to Jesus. No time like the present to teach my child the art of freely giving to God what He has given to you, right?

Cotter loudly said, "No! I don't want to. I keep it." The row of college girls in front of me begin to snicker. The plate stopped at us. Cotter kept his quarter clutched in his hand and took a swipe at the green bills held in front of him.

"But Cotter," I quietly explained, "we give Jesus our money because we love Him."

Without any social inhibition or respect for the morning worship service and just as the offertory came to an end, Cotter loudly proclaimed in his shrill toddler voice, "But I don't wuv Jesus!"

The row of college girls completely lost it. I even heard snorting. And I hoped they offered a sympathetic prayer for the battle-weary mom who had produced a little heathen. We must keep our sense of humor, sister-soldiers, for times like these. We desperately need it.

"But seriously," Supermom argued, "does God really expect you to deal with these selfish children every day? I mean, they're exhausting. They regularly publicly humiliate you! Don't you remember this week's trip to Walmart when they all screamed at the same time and one of them shattered the glass bottle of pickles on the floor? You deserve better than this. You need to get involved in something where you can be appreciated for who you are."

And I listened to her for a while. I had talents after all. I could remember the time when I wore makeup every day and pretty heels to church, when I felt the thrill of teaching in a classroom and coordinating school programs, when my clothes were ironed and clean—at the same time—, and when I regularly heard positive feedback from others for my gifts. What happened to those days? Now I mostly got looks of sympathy and assurances that others were praying for me.

So what rights has God actually given me?

When God laid all my sins on Jesus and punished Him for it, I gained a new position as His beloved child. Because of Jesus, I am now called an heir, a beloved daughter of the high King of heaven. I have full access to His throne of grace in the name of Jesus. I have forgiveness of my sin through Jesus. I have the promise of heaven because of Jesus.

Excuse me while I shout a few "Hallelujahs!"

Every single claim I have to God and His heaven has nothing to do with who I am, how good I am, how much I read the Bible, where I attend church, or how my kids turn out. It has everything to do with Jesus. When God looks at me now, He sees His Son standing in my place. So the position in Heaven I have as His child was not earned by me at all. This was His gift to me because of the obedience of His Son.

To put it bluntly, I don't have any rights outside of my position in Jesus. None. Nada. Zip.

Supermom was not happy about my discovery. She's greedy like that.

If I don't have any rights to appreciative, obedient children, a doting husband, and a good night's sleep, what was the real issue here?

And then I knew. It was contentment. I wasn't content in this place where God had me. I was so busy looking back with longing to fulfilling years of ministry and looking forward with yearning to the years my children wouldn't be so draining that I wasn't seeing the beauty of today.

TRENCH CONTENTMENT

Pride had robbed me of contentment. Real contentment is my realizing that God has provided every single thing I need for my present happiness—*everything* right now!

I had forgotten that one of the most profoundly beautiful experiences in life is the seasons. Every season has its beginning, its middle, and, inevitably, its end. My favorite season is fall. I love that first snap of crisp, cold air and its relief from summer heat, the excitement of spying that first orange leaf, and the breathtaking beauty of a valley of red, orange, yellow, purple, and green trees standing in praise to their Creator against a turquoise-blue sky. I also feel sadness at the end of the fall season as the last few leaves flutter to the ground, a lifeless brown. But then my heart begins to anticipate the excitement of that first snowfall and the beauty of a world in sparkling white. And so it goes.

The lesson for me is clear. Life has seasons. Each season has its beginning, its fullness, its end. Each element is beautiful in its own way, designed by its Creator for a purpose. Each element is necessary in preparing the way for what is to come. The leaves fall to the ground to allow the trees to rest in the winter in preparation for new growth in the spring.

And think about it, the seasons spur us to action. When winter is coming, we winterize our homes and vehicles, purchase mittens, and put away the sand toys in the backyard. Spring cleaning also came about for a reason. Something in us wants to be rid of the heaviness of winter and the stuff we've accumulated. Living within the framework of time is a gift, if we choose to see it that way.

A wise man once remarked to me that the grass is only greener where you water it. Wow. Now isn't that the truth? If I stand in the sticky, stinky trench of momhood wishing for the sweet freedoms of singlehood or the promise of quiet times when my children are at school in the future, those eras will most definitely appear better to me than the moment I'm in. But if I water the grass in my momhood trench, it will become green and lush with beauty. It will offer cool relief on a hot day and softness beneath my feet.

I need to be fully here in my baby-toddler-preschool trench with joy, with gratefulness for previous busy singlehood ministry, and with anticipation of the new opportunities of ministry when my kids get older.

Patience, true patience, is not cheerfully waiting on God to give me what I want. Rather it is a complete submission to God's will for me, in every circumstance, in every relationship, in every season.

But for now, in this season of momhood, I need to look for the beauty of it. I need to embrace the moments of rocking my toddlers and singing songs to soothe them. I need to stop and really share their wonder as they hold a worm for the first time and feel it desperately wriggling to escape their sticky hands. I need to take the time to snap a picture to remind myself of the beauty God has given my life right now.

And when I find the joy of the present gifts of God, I can help my children find joy too.

The past is over. The future is yet to come. But right now, I have the opportunity of living in my present—inglorious battle trench that it is—with no regrets. Nothing lasts forever except the grace and love of God. His love is season-less.

I should most certainly remember the past—remember the gifts of God; remember my weaknesses; remember His strength.

And I should most certainly look with great anticipation to the future He has for me. Only He knows what that is, but He did tell me that it's good.

> *For I know the thoughts that I think toward you,*
> *saith the Lord, thoughts of peace, and not of evil,*
> *to give you an expected end. (Jeremiah 29:11)*

> *Being confident of this very thing, that he which*
> *hath begun a good work in you will perform it*
> *until the day of Jesus Christ. (Philippians 1:6)*

He's doing a good work in me. He's doing one in you too. He's still helping me chop away at my trunk of pride. I confess, it's still there, and it still sends out shoots in the hope of re-growing limbs. Supermom tends her tree with ferocious attention. But by

God's grace, we can become excellent Swordswomen, radically amputating and maiming Supermom's most prized possession.

He gives us a choice of how we respond to His conviction. When we resist His conviction for our sin, we set ourselves on a downward spiral of apathy, selfishness, and destruction, like the Pharisees and like Saul.

But when we humble ourselves, confess our pride, and walk completely dependent on Him, we find ourselves in the company of people like David, like the woman caught in adultery. We find ourselves, all of us, at the feet of Jesus.

We find ourselves forgiven. Loved.

WHAT ABOUT ME?

1. Spend some time praising God for His Word—the powerful Sword He has entrusted to you. Consciously elevate His Word in your mind over the advice of others, over selfish philosophies to get what you want, and over Hollywood's emotional fodder of entitlement. Set God's Word in the place of honor and authority in your heart and mind. Fight to the death any other thought process that would try to take its place in your life.

2. What sin patterns in your life has God used your children to reveal in you? Please be painfully honest. Make a list and then open your Bible and deal with them one by one.

3. When you sin and are confronted for it, either by God or someone else, whose response is more like yours, Saul's or David's? Do you tend to rationalize your sin, excuse it, or blame someone else for it? Or do you immediately humble yourself, acknowledge your sin, and prostrate yourself before the Lord begging for His mercy and forgiveness? I know this is painful, but please take time to consider your response. It will give you great insight into the true condition of your heart.

4. All of us have a tree trunk of pride in our lives. It's the lifeblood of our Supermoms. How has pride manifested itself in your life, in your relationships, and with your

children? If necessary, take the time to do some radical amputations, confessing your sin, and reconciling your precious relationships.

5. Do you struggle with trench contentment? Begin a list of the simple gifts God gives you each day in your trench. Spend time focusing on His love for you manifested in His gifts to you. Your circumstances probably won't change right away. But your heart can when it finds joy in God's personal, intimate love for you.

Thy voice shall bid the tempter flee,
And I shall stand complete in Thee.[1]

Aaron R. Wolfe

Chapter Five
The Battle of Expectations

Let's face it. The standard of success for females in our current society is set rather high. Society says we should be independent, free-spirited, driven, and motivated. Socially, we're to be quick-witted, gracious, and possess a clever sense of humor. We should be able to handle a career as well as manage a home and rear well-adjusted children. We should remain sexually appealing at all times. We should be emotionally stable and never appear incompetent in any area lest someone be tempted to think we are not up to the task.

And as Christian women, there are more standards to meet—higher standards. We should have a tamed tongue, a gracious spirit, a home always open to hospitality, a loving attitude, a non-existent temper, and the ultimate goal—to be like Jesus Christ.

Supermom tells us that in order to be successful, we must meet these obligations of womanhood. She whispers that we should pursue excellence and never settle for less from ourselves. After all, she counters, the Bible does say you should "approve things that are excellent" (Philippians 1:10). She gets us to focus on all the good things we should be to our husband, children, church, and friends. It sounds harmless. In fact, it actually sounds pretty good.

But it's destructive.

So I made a list. I wrote out all the expectations I felt were upon me as a wife, as a mother, as a member of my church, as part of a full-time ministry, and as a friend. That list was long. And it was made up of good things! What Christian wife shouldn't want to support her husband? What Christian mom shouldn't want to teach orderliness and cleanliness to her children? What Christian sister shouldn't want to be sensitive to the needs of others in her church? Each goal on my list could be easily rationalized and was therefore given its place on my list. Almost all of them could even be biblically justified in some way.

If you have a few minutes, stop right now and make your list. Write it out. What expectations do you feel have been placed on you by your husband, your children, your parents, your church, your career, and your friends? Be very specific.

And then make another list. Write out the personal expectations that you have placed upon yourself. To you, what are the obligations of your role as a Christian, as a mother, and as a woman?

I have a feeling your list has good things on it. Mine did too. It listed things I wanted to do, and altogether, it described the God-honoring Christian woman I wanted to be.

And then I made a huge, devastating mistake. I took my list and tried to practically implement those expectations into my life. Remember I'm a to-do list kind of girl. I like a clear set of goals, because I love the feeling of success that comes when I attain them. I'm that selfish. I have the same tendencies as the Pharisees; I take God's Word and twist it to make myself look good.

THE SIN

My husband is aware of my moods. He's aware of my frustrations and my joys. He loves me fully and completely. Inside my wedding ring he had inscribed "inside out love." And he has lived this out. He has loved me through changes, moves, ups, downs, health, sickness, babies, pounds, and emotions. He committed to a studied attempt to "dwell with . . . knowledge" or understanding (1 Peter 3:7) with his wife. For this I'm deeply, eternally grateful. He's one of God's precious gifts to me.

The downside of having a husband who is in tune with you means you can't really get by with anything. He knows when I'm angry. He knows when I'm sad. He knows when I feel discouraged. He knows when my spirit is peaceful. He knows when I'm being stubborn, prideful, selfish, and resentful. And he calls me on it.

When I dived in to meeting all the expectations of a married, Christian mother in the ministry, he immediately became wary. He watched me become frustrated and discouraged and impatient at home with him as well as with our children when they didn't help me accomplish those expectations. He saw me walk further and further into bondage to those expectations.

One of many examples of my failed attempt to meet my expectations is in the area of hospitality. I married a man who loves people. He has a deep compassion for people and prefers to be surrounded by others. Unfortunately for him, he married a girl who prefers solitude, fuzzy socks, and a good book.

On my list under the expectations of my husband, I had written "be hospitable"—a worthy and biblical expectation. Romans 12:13 says we are to be "given to hospitality." Add to that command the fact that my husband wanted us to train our children to have compassion for others, and I had a firm expectation. So in classic Supermom style, I determined I'd do just that.

She's like that. She takes a biblical truth and twists it to meet her own selfish needs, like Satan did with Eve. He took the truth of what God said and twisted it to appeal to Eve's selfish desire for knowledge. Read Genesis 3:1–6 for the story.

So Supermom took the biblical command to be hospitable and twisted it to meet my selfish need for praise and approval.

I carefully planned out the times when people could come to our house. I was obsessed with doing this well. I cleaned, organized, shopped, cooked, and generally became a terror to my family. I was impatient, rude, and intolerant of my children's inability to keep themselves and their rooms clean. I was also resentful of their insensitivity to what I was trying to do. I'm trying to be hospitable here! Why wasn't anyone helping me clean this house? I was a driven woman.

The problem was I was driven by Supermom, not the Holy Spirit.

What I didn't immediately see was that I wasn't actually trying to be hospitable. I was trying to set up the circumstances of inviting people to my home to get a few pats on the back and impress my friends by looking like I was being hospitable—just like those Pharisees did.

One night Bobby firmly pulled me aside during the cleaning marathon when the ETA of our guests was about thirty minutes. I was panicking at the state of a previously cleaned bathroom and was getting ready to express my anger to the child who had apparently completely missed the toilet and then pumped out the foam soap to make bubble skyscrapers on the cabinet. And who had slimed the doorknob?

He said simply, "Robin, you're not walking in the Spirit." I offered a quick justification of my poor attitude. "People should be able to use a clean bathroom at our house!"

His response shook me to my core. "Robin, I don't care if the bathroom is cleaned. Neither do our guests, and neither does God. What we care about is that your heart is right with God."

I was angry at first. I had fully justified my sinful actions. Humility was far from me, but I knew he was right. I had missed the mark completely.

I wallowed in self-pity for a few days after that. Supermom had her questions ready for me. "Will you always be a failure? Why can't you be successful at anything? You can't even be hospitable the right way. Bobby's so disappointed in you. You can't even pull off having a few people over peacefully. But it's just not fair that he has these expectations for you. After all, it shows loving care and honor for others when they come to a clean home."

"And really," she whispered, "is it fair of God to ask you to have people over all the time when you have young children?"

Supermom always leads our minds to question the goodness of God. Remember she takes her cue from Satan.

That's when I realized I was in a spiritual battle . . . again. This wasn't about Bobby, my children's irresponsibility, my house, or our guests. This was a showdown between the Holy Spirit and Supermom in my heart. Battle lines were drawn.

THE BATTLE

It was time to pick up my Sword.

Supermom needled me. "Is it fair of God to ask this of you?"

The Sword says exactly what God asks of me.

> *He hath shewed thee, O man, what is good; and what doth the Lord require of thee, but to do justly, and to love mercy, and to walk humbly with thy God? (Micah 6:8)*

The Sword also offers a firm warning.

> *Take heed that ye do not your alms before men, to be seen of them: otherwise ye have no reward of your Father which is in heaven. (Matthew 6:1)*

Supermom whispered, "Look, the time will come for this. Just give up on this for now. While your children are young, surely God doesn't expect you to be hospitable when it's impossible to keep a clean house!"

And the Sword said, "Therefore to him that knoweth to do good, and doeth it not, to him it is sin" (James 4:17).

"But if you are hospitable with a dirty house," she countered, "your guests won't feel comfortable."

And the Spirit replied that a clean house isn't necessary for my guests to be blessed. Instead the Sword says, "Beloved, let us love one another: for love is of God; and every one that loveth is born of God, and knoweth God. He that loveth not knoweth not God; for God is love" (1 John 4:7–8).

So Supermom whimpered, "Well, I think it's loving for guests to have a clean toilet to use."

And the Sword said, "By this shall all men know that ye are my disciples, if ye have love one to another" (John 13:35).

And she left me alone—for then.

I learned then that when God asks me to be hospitable, He's asking me to minister to others from a heart of love that He has given to me. Nowhere does He ask me to impress them.

Supermom says the bathrooms must be spotless, the dinner a perfect temperature, the toys put away, the floor mopped, the children dressed appropriately, and my makeup applied before true hospitality can happen.

God says all that is necessary is for my heart to be in tune with Him, allowing His love to flow out of my heart straight to my guests.

Believe me, after the yelling and rushing around before guests came to my house, my children avoided me, my husband was frustrated, and I was just generally angry. And then, hypocritically, I was kind and loving to my guests, teaching my children it was okay to be unloving to family members as long as those outside of your family saw you as gracious and kind. What a lie!

What was I really teaching my children?

- I was teaching them by my own example that I cared more about what people thought about me than I did about loving them.

- I was teaching them that our needs for affirmation can be met by people and that we should work hard to earn it.

- I was teaching them that the reason we reach out to people is to make ourselves feel good.

Wow! What kind of mother was I? A sinful one. That much was absolutely clear to me. If any of our guests were actually ministered to by me during those years in my home, it was a merciful miracle of God.

God meant for me:

- to use His command for hospitality to surround my guests with His love

- to use hospitality to teach my children how to love others the way Jesus loves them

- to use hospitality to teach my children that loving others is a free gift we give to them, expecting nothing in return

In no way are we dependent on others to give us affirmation because our joy and security are found in God alone.

In those early years of our marriage, Bobby gave my sinful nature a name. He calls her "Jenny" since Jennifer is my first name. To this day when guests are scheduled to arrive at our home, he usually checks with me—with a wary smile—to see if Jenny is coming too. We're all much happier when I don't invite her.

BACK TO THE LIST

Remember those lists of expectations we made? Let's look at them again.

When I looked over my list, I came to the quick realization that most of the expectations I carried were ones I had put on myself.

Your answers—if you've written honestly—will reveal a wealth of information about your heart and motives. Mine sure did, especially when I began comparing them to the fruit of the Spirit.

Our lists of "obligations" can also be entitled "My Definition of Success." In other words, if we don't meet the expectations before us, we will struggle with the feeling of failure for the rest of our life. And who among us has ever satisfactorily met all the expectations of our heart? Is this what God wants for us? To live in a spirit of failure and frustration?

GOD'S EXPECTATIONS

We are all familiar with that list of godly womanhood in Proverbs 31, and we all have mixed emotions about that woman. Seriously, I can't wait to meet that mother in heaven who gave this description of a godly woman to her son. I have a few choice questions for her. Talk about heavy expectations!

There are other lists of desirable qualities given in the New Testament as well, but let's get to the core of them all.

> Moreover it is required in stewards, that a man be found faithful. But with me it is a very small thing that I should be judged of you, or of man's judgment: yea, I judge not mine own self. For I know nothing by myself; yet am I not hereby justified: but he that judgeth me is the Lord. (1 Corinthians 4:2–4)

That's a tongue-tripping set of verses for sure. But what does it mean?

In our modern speech, this simply means that you and I are to be found faithful in pursuing God and reflecting His light to others. We don't have to waste time trying to determine if somebody else is a *successful* woman, and it doesn't matter if other moms judge or criticize us. We know that without God, we are nothing and can attain nothing good.

Successfully meeting a list of obligations or merely fulfilling a role is not going to justify us before our Father in heaven. No. We have to know God to know what He wants us to be. When we finally realize that His primary goal for us is to reflect the love of Christ to others, then everything in our lives becomes a tool in His hand to that end. Even the drudgery of laundry brings joy because we know God is teaching us patience and giving us yet another opportunity to be faithful in loving our family.

If I am driven to find success by fulfilling a checklist of obligations, I find that I become incredibly self-focused. If I merely define myself by how I accomplish the role given to me, I am seriously missing God's point. In fact I am becoming pharisaical, and we all know what Jesus said about them in John 12:43. They were so religious about meeting good obligations that they missed the Savior in front of their faces. Let us be warned, sisters.

I do believe that defining our role as a wife or mother is a good starting point. We need to know what gifts God has given us, what responsibilities He has entrusted us with, and what the areas are in which He wants to stretch us beyond our comfortable capabilities. For me one of those areas was hospitality.

If we are driven to meet someone's expectation of us rather than love God, we fail; if we find comfort in successfully fulfilling our own expectations of ourselves, we have failed again, and either way, what a wasted life that would be.

Supermom wants us to take the detour off the path to God. She wants us to get so wrapped up in doing good things that we never find God. That would be like spending two hours preparing a good meal and never taking a bite of it. I realize that's pretty normal for those of us who spend mealtime cutting up food into tiny bites, cleaning up spilled milk, feeding other little people, and answering a trillion frivolous questions from busy motor mouths. You know how you feel after a meal like that. Tired, frazzled, and a little bit frustrated that you never were able to enjoy the food you prepared.

Our role is simply a tool that God is using in our lives to show us how much we need Him, to show us how much He loves us, and to show us how faithful He is.

Successfully fulfilling our roles does not define our success as a woman. In fact, no matter how much energy we put into meeting our obligations, we will always come up short. We will always have some area in which we find that our self-sufficiency is not enough. As frustrating as this is to those of us who are goal oriented and relish the satisfaction of completing to-do lists, this inevitable personal failure is by the design of our merciful, loving God.

He never intended for us to merely fulfill a role in life. He wants more for us. He wants us to enjoy a thriving, real, intense, and powerful relationship with Him. God wants a relationship with me. God wants a relationship with you. He wants to talk to us every day. He wants to interact with us, to listen to us, to share with us, to love us, and to lead us to the greatest joy we've ever known. No other human being could ever love us that much.

When we are driven to fulfill a role, we are actually driven by a desire to feel good about ourselves and to look successful to others. Okay, that's called *pride*, and pride will *separate* us from God, not draw us to Him.

> God resisteth the proud, but giveth grace unto the
> humble. (James 4:6)

When we use the role God has given us as a tool to develop a deeper relationship with Him, we begin to be driven by an intense love for our God because we see His sovereign Hand in a very personal way, loving us, shaping us, and molding us to be more like Jesus, our Savior.

MOTIVE AND MODERN IDOLATRY

It is our motive that is in question here. Remember Hebrews 4:12?

> For the word of God is quick, and powerful, and
> sharper than any twoedged sword, piercing even to
> the dividing asunder of soul and spirit, . . . and is
> a discerner of the thoughts and intents of the heart.

So what are the thoughts and intents of my heart? Of your heart? These are personal questions, for sure. What motivates us to fulfill those expectations on our list?

Jesus dealt with a rich young man about the motives of his heart. The young man was one of good character in the eyes of other religious people of his time. It became immediately apparent that he considered himself pretty successful as well. So Jesus went straight to his heart, past the list of fulfilled obligations this good, rich, young man was hiding behind. Jesus asked him to choose between his wealth and a relationship with Christ.

Jesus asked him to sell everything he had and to give to the poor and then to follow Him. The young man's selfish motives were revealed by his choice. He walked away from Christ and chose to cling to his reputation and successful business ventures instead. You can read his story in Matthew 19:16–30 and Mark 10:17–31.

Merely conforming to a high standard of behavior as a mom does not mean that you are pleasing God or even that you know God at all.

Yikes! Are we doing the same thing? Are we choosing to pour our energies into becoming supermoms rather than pursuing Christ himself?

The Bible teaches that the pursuit of anything other than pursuing God is empty and pointless. In fact, it is idolatry. It is the same kind of idolatry we picture in our heads when we read about those foolish Israelites turning from God and offering sacrifices to statues of stones. It's modern idolatry. You and I might not spend time kneeling before a golden calf, but I confess to you I've found myself bowing down to the idol of my own pride time and time again.

My most attended-to idol is certainly myself. My own Supermom does everything she can to take my focus, my attention, my worship, and my loyalties from God. She wants to sit on His throne in my heart. Every time I lose a battle with her, every time I neglect to pick up God's Word and defeat her, I'm bowing to her in worship.

Supermom is indeed evil. We know that. She wants us to focus on her and our list of good deeds rather than pursue God. She wants to earn kudos and some pats on the back for her amazing accomplishments in the face of difficulty. She wants to make the other girls jealous, and she masterfully employs guilt as her persuasion. After all, what mom doesn't want to be a good one?

Many years ago a chapel speaker at my Christian college made the statement that the greatest sin of any Christian was living independently from God. In other words, if we allow ourselves to be a slave to the yoke of religious obligation, then we'll only strive to fulfill a role as a woman. But if we recognize that our role and our ministry are merely instruments to humble us so that we can draw closer to God, then our success will be measured by how well we know God. We will not be measured by how our house looks, how many people we entertain, or how well-mannered our children are.

Shouldn't we rather be driven by the love of our God? Is that really possible in the world of momhood or of housewife?

Yes! I can keep my house clean because I love God. There is no sense of heavy obligation in that pure motive but to abundantly pour out my energies in joyfully fulfilling the service He has given me.

I do struggle with the selfish desire to succeed as a mom. My motives include both selfish and unselfish reasons. I want my children to love God. I want my husband to love me. I want my friends to be impressed because my house is clean and well decorated. I certainly want to *appear* Christlike, whether I really am or not.

So God faithfully provides opportunities to show me that I can't succeed the way I want to. He has revealed to me that I have the wrong definition of "success." He has called me to love Him first of all. He wants my heart, my mind, my body, and then He has called me to be faithful. So my goal is not to raise perfect kids; my goal is to love Him. In loving Him, I'll be diligent with the time He gives me with my children so that I can show them by my example a mom who loves God with all her heart and lives every single day walking in His Spirit.

I'm not suggesting that we let the dishes pile up in the sink for days, neglect our personal appearance, or allow our children to run wild while we meditate on Scripture. Remember we're called to be faithful with the responsibilities that He has entrusted to us. And after a few months of motherhood, we all learned that we can actually do the dishes, make dinner, mediate a battle of wills between the children, and pray simultaneously.

I am saying that we need to passionately pursue our God and be consumed with His Person and His Word. Then, and only then, will we be able to rightly fulfill our God-given roles because we will know Him and what He created us to be and do.

A mom whose life is consumed by fulfilling her role may look like a Supermom. But far better is a mom who rests in Jesus and consistently displays the stunning beauty of the fruit of the Spirit, bringing glory to her God, rather than herself.

He created me to love Him. Then He gave me my role as a mother to show my children His love and show them how to fight their sinful natures with the Sword so that they too can be free from empty, pointless, selfish expectations. And He gave me the Sword of His Word to do battle with Supermom and win while they watch.

Thoughtfully consider the poem on the next page written by a friend that captures the death of her expectations. I hope it captures ours as well.

OF GLORY

She worshiped misconceptions
thrust upon her by
the lifelong prophecy that she
"will do great things for God."
And has imagined
all this time
building castles
for that coming Kingdom.
Therefore
it shocks
and falls as Negative
at first
when her Lord
permits—
No!
Pursues
her into caverns
deep within the earth
where seemingly alone
she wrestles with the weight
of what must have been and
Truth.
Yet for good
All this is done
That all men might say not
"She did great things for Him."
But
"Great things for her were done."[2]

Indeed. God's greatest work for me is not what He accomplishes *through* me. It's His loving transformation *in* me, pursuing me until His perfect work is complete within my heart.

How deep the love of God.

WHAT ABOUT ME?

1. It may be that you don't feel driven at all to be anything to anyone. Maybe you believe you're free from others' expectations of you. Perhaps, but consider. Remember that our Supermoms often tempt us to sin at one extreme or the other of God's plan of rest. I'm most often tempted to overachieve for selfish recognition. The other extreme is to underachieve so that no one will ever expect anything from you or me, and therefore we won't ever feel like a failure. A fear of failure is motivated by self-preservation which stems from selfishness too. I know sisters who must battle on this side of the tree of pride. You may be in the trenches with them. Either extreme is motivated by our selfishness and pride and can be battled against with the same powerful verses of our Sword. Which trench do you battle in?

2. If you haven't already, make a list of the expectations you and others have of you. Include family, church, work, and personal expectations. Consider your list carefully. This is the list that Supermom can use to enslave you to a selfish pursuit of success. Do you feel enslaved already? Have you found yourself pursuing success in any of the items on your list rather than or more than resting in Christ?

3. If you find yourself enslaved in any way, don't waste any time feeling guilty about it or trying harder. Simply confess your idolatry, receive His forgiveness, and pursue resting in Jesus. Fill your mind with His Word and allow His Spirit to begin working *through* you rather than you wearing yourself out trying to work *for* God.

4. Choose one area in which you especially struggle. Write down the arguments your Supermom uses against you to rationalize your selfish pursuit of success in that area. Remember my battle with Supermom over my motive for hospitality? Write out yours. Use verses to counteract every single argument or justification your Supermom throws at you. Fight her. Don't let her win. Her victory is your destruction.

*ay low every rebel lust;
let no vile passion resist thy holy war.*[1]

Valley of Vision

Chapter Six
The Battle for Control

Okay, I admit it. I'm a perfectionist at heart. I struggle with the internal drive that things should be organized and in their proper place and that it is my God-given and Robin-desired goal to make it that way.

In other words, I like control. I like to feel that I'm the master of my surroundings, my ministry, and my responsibilities. In fact I selfishly thrive on responsibilities because they give me the opportunity to shine.

I'm the ultimate multitasker. And yes, I take pride in it.

When I began losing control of my surroundings, my house, my new ministry of motherhood, my children . . . well, I crashed. I crashed hard.

You know how you feel when you are operating on a mere three hours of interrupted sleep and how utterly hopeless you are because you know that the next twenty-four hours won't be any different than the twenty-four hours before.

I felt that lack of control when my twins emptied two bookshelves of their contents and then lay in the shelves like they were bunk beds, and when they raided their brother's underwear drawer and wore his tighty-whities on their heads the rest of the week as helmets.

I felt it when Caeden, to avoid eating his banana, sneaked into the bathroom and flushed it down the toilet—peel and all. No amount of plunging would fix that state of affairs. Bobby and I had to actually pull up the toilet from the floor and retrieve the decomposing banana from the porcelain basin. Disgusting.

I felt it when I discovered that a sticky brown Cotter and his eight-month-old brother had eaten most of a bag of Hershey's Kisses on the kitchen floor. "Don't worry, Mommy," Cotter assured me. "I share!"

I felt it when Cotter smeared handfuls of Vaseline into the twins' hair and no amount of cornstarch or Dawn dishwashing soap would remove it—for days.

I felt it when I had carefully saved my pennies for my glorious ten-foot, pre-lit artificial Christmas tree, and the day after we put it up the kids climbed it to the top, rendering it forever lopsided.

I felt it when I tried and failed to teach my kids that food goes into their mouths . . . not their ears, their nose, or on the floor.

I felt it when I came to the sad realization that the dried oatmeal on the floor would stay there—yes, not only stay there, but would be joined by greasy spaghetti, mud, and a few dust bunnies as well, and just might not *ever* be cleaned up. Ever.

I felt it when I focused on the books all over the floor, the crooked tree, the food-covered child, or the dried oatmeal. I began to realize that I give permission to Supermom to beat me on the head for my failure. I then give my consent to feelings of guilt and frustration at my lack of control over my surroundings and my children's actions. This frustration keeps me from viewing each situation as an opportunity to honor my Father by just being faithful in the calling He has given to me.

As long as Supermom is acknowledged in my heart, I give her the power to whisper "Failure!" in my ear. The longer I go throughout a day listening to her whisper, the more control over my spirit I give to her, and soon I've allowed her to skew my thinking so that I'm feeling sorry for myself and angry at my children for not letting me control them.

The struggle in my heart is always for control. I know that my flesh—that wicked Supermom—wants control over my emotions and thoughts. I know that God's Spirit is at war with Supermom every day in every situation, for mastery.

Supermom wants to be in charge of every situation and every person in my life, and she fuels my selfishness at every opportunity. The Spirit fights back by empowering me with the same power He gave to Jesus to fight the devil's temptations. The same power. Think about it. You have the same power to fight temptations as Jesus did. Wow.

THE GLORY THIEF

Supermom wants the glory. She wants attention. She wants the credit, and she'll do everything she can to steal glory that belongs to God alone. Remember, she wants to be like God. (Isaiah 14:12–15)

A glory thief is the embodiment of selfishness. She's someone who by some word, action, attitude, or spiritual deception seeks to steal the glory that belongs only to God. Many glory thieves are intentional in their methods and therefore easy to identify. We see them on TV manipulating money from loyal listeners, in business using their God-given gifts to work their way to the top of their organizations, and in pulpits amassing large crowds to hear them pontificate. Rightfully so, we observe these extremists in horror.

But the heart is "deceitfully wicked," and we are so easily self-deceived. While I point my finger in disbelief and shake my head in sorrow at public examples of the glory thief, I amiably pass over my own sinful tendencies and the grasping of my own evil flesh at glory due to my God alone.

What exactly does a glory thief look like?

- *She gives honor where it is not due.* She flatters, manipulates, and uses others to achieve some sort of selfish gain.

- *She withholds honor where it is due.* Believing that people owe her, she overlooks the humble, meek, and servant-hearted around her, even when they are serving her, because, after all, she's entitled to their service.

- *She takes personal ownership for the work of God in her life and the lives of those she influences.* Rather than understand her position as a humble steward entrusted with a call, a ministry, children, resources, and spiritual gifts, she credits herself for the upkeep of these good gifts. In her heart, she has displaced God's position as owner and set herself up as queen. She lives as if God actually owes her for the excellent job she is doing.

- *She lacks a grateful spirit.* After all, it's everyone else who should be grateful to *her.*

- *She reacts in anger when God sovereignly intervenes in her life.* When God allows tragedy, demotion, spiritual confrontation, deferred hope, or some other reminder that she isn't in charge, she shakes her fist in His face and asks "Why?" as if He answers to her, rather than submit to His authority and rest in His goodness.

- *She is jealous of the God-given gifts of others.* Rather than accept joyfully the gifts He has given to her, she resents what He has withheld.

- *She is fearful and insecure.* She makes decisions driven by a fear of personal failure or weakness, rather than in defense of or for the magnification of the good character of God.

- *She is distrustful of others.* She wrongfully judges their motives, fearing she will be displaced or replaced.

- *She pours forth a harsh, critical spirit toward those who do not agree with her.* She sets herself up as the standard to follow, rather than understand the beauty of grace God has extended to her in her state of sinfulness.

- *She resents any form of personal and/or spiritual account-ability by her authorities.* She doesn't need to answer to anyone but herself, demonstrating a complete lack of understanding of her own sinful tendencies.

- *She exhibits the subtle attitude that her calling, her position, her position, her character, her family, and more make her somehow more important to God and His Kingdom than the stewardship He has given to others.* Pride blinds her to her foolishness.

- *She lacks genuine love for the body of Christ.* She tends to take the *long-suffering* approach of *putting up* with the shortcomings and faults of others, while silently judging them in her heart.

- *She pridefully defends her honor when confronted.* Humility brings glory to God. Pride grasps at glory for herself.

At some point in your spiritual journey, I'm sure your Supermom will tempt you to steal glory that belongs to God, just as she does me. Be on the lookout. Remember the words of 1 Peter 5:8–11:

> *Be sober, be vigilant; because your adversary the devil, as a roaring lion, walketh about, seeking whom he may devour: Whom resist stedfast in the faith, knowing that the same afflictions are accomplished in your brethren that are in the world. But the God of all grace, who hath called us unto his eternal glory by Christ Jesus, after that ye have suffered a while, make you perfect, stablish, strengthen, settle you.* **To him be glory** *and dominion for ever and ever. Amen.*

BROKEN BONES

I love Proverbs. It is full of wisdom and practical solutions to everyday battles between my flesh and my spirit. While there are many verses in Proverbs that address the issue of control, this one stands out to me because of the contrast it presents.

> *A merry heart doeth good like a medicine: but a*
> *broken spirit drieth the bones. (Proverbs 17:22)*

A merry heart is strong and functions properly in relationship to the rest of the body. It is full of joy that overflows into the entire body just as a broken spirit also affects the body, but in a very negative way. In a medical sense, the central marrow of the bones is the primary location of blood cell production. So bones that are dried out aren't producing adequate life-giving blood for the body. There is no mistake in God's analogy here. A spirit that is not under the control of God's Spirit is broken and will eventually destroy itself and the very body that possesses it.

Notice that the consequences of the merry heart and the broken spirit are not necessarily limited to the one who owns them. They also affect everyone around them. So the state of my heart does *me* either good or evil, but it also directly affects my husband and children, my church, my neighbors.

There's nothing like living 24/7 with three children under the age of two to give you a "broken spirit." If I focus on the work they create for me, what is not getting accomplished around the house, and the number of days (yes, days!) it has been since my last long shower, my spirit gets "broken" rather quickly.

But when my heart is resting in the Lord and the joy overflows to my attitude, it also overflows and becomes a healing stream of God's power to my husband and children. Good medicine allows the body to heal as well as relieves pain. Is that what I do with my husband and children? Or do I more often dry out their bones (as well as my own) with my pouting broken spirit?

I hate to admit this, but I can do a good pout. Usually it is manifested in a cold, resentful silence. My husband dreads it. He calls it my "evil eye." He says that at times I actually yell at him with my eyes without ever uttering a sound from my mouth. My children have noticed it too. They give me confused glances and become cranky and disobedient. My two-year-old even commented one time on my pouting spirit. "Mommy," he said seriously, "you are bweing dipicult."

If my toddler can pick up on a resentful spirit, it must be pretty obvious! Since we mothers are on a constant stage before our children's watchful eyes, it is crucial that we don't let Supermom win the battle for control.

WHO'S IN CHARGE?

Does Supermom (my sinful nature) or the Spirit of God control me?

- Do I get irritated when my husband must stay late at the office, or do I take the opportunity to thank God for his job and how he provides for me?

- Do I get frustrated when my child disobeys me because it inconveniences me and publicly proves I'm not in control, or does it grieve my spirit because I see that my child just lost the struggle for control going on in his heart?

- Do I feel angry when my mental schedule is interrupted by the needs of my husband or children, or is my spirit submissive to opportunities to minister to them no matter the time of day or night?

These are the questions the Holy Spirit has asked me—questions He has convicted me with.

These are issues of the heart. The battle for control begins at the heart. I'm not even talking about external actions like lashing out verbally at our husbands or children or giving them the "evil eye."

I'm talking about our hearts. If we lose the battle for control in our hearts, then these hurtful things will certainly follow because they are the fruits of our sinful nature. But if we defeat the power of Supermom and submit to God's sovereignty in every single circumstance, then the fruit of the Spirit will naturally flow from us with little effort on our part.

Bramble bushes grow thorns. Apple trees grow apples. Out of a sinful heart flows sinful action. But a Spirit-filled heart can't help but bear the Spirit's fruit that we read about in Galatians 5:22–23.

Our husband and children are the finest judges of who we really are. If we're really serious about finding out who we are, we should ask them to tell us. You'll probably be surprised to see yourself through the eyes of those closest to you. I was. Our very best efforts to present ourselves as mature, successful wives and mothers to our peers fall flat before the honest scrutiny of those with whom we live.

If you do ask your family members for areas that you need to work on spiritually—and I highly recommend it—, prepare to be humbled. You should probably have a pen and paper handy to write down the list along with a box of tissue for your tears.

Commit to receiving their comments with grace and love no matter how deeply they plunge into your heart or how wrong you think they may be. Remember that a very telling mark of a growing Christian is the ability to receive with wisdom and humility the critical comments of others. I'm still growing into this one. Sometimes I think I need a tongue clamp to keep me quiet when being criticized . . . um, I mean, when I'm being *encouraged to grow spiritually*.

Even more telling is your ability as a Christian to express gratefulness to those individuals for loving you enough to help you grow to love like Jesus does. Seriously, when was the last time I thanked my husband for confronting me about my desire to have things my way?

I'm going to ask you to make another list. Yes, I know. I love lists because there's something about putting my vague, scrambled thoughts down on paper that makes me see them for what they really are and forces me to deal with their brutal honesty. I hope seeing your thoughts in black and white will help you too.

Make your own list of situations that put you in the position of fighting the battle for control between your flesh and spirit. This is the list of the situations that tempt you to react in selfishness.

My list includes food thrown on the floor necessitating me crawling under the table to scrub the floor on my hands and knees, or dirty clothes that can't seem to find their way to the laundry hamper leaving me to examine and even sniff the garments to determine if they qualify for the washing machine. And what about the wet, used towels on the bathroom floor? We have *hooks*, people!

These things make the muscles in my neck stiffen. My first Supermom response is to resent the action and the people who dared to treat me as a mere house slave. After all, Supermom deserves better than to have to scrape gross food from the floor and pick up dirty clothes. Why won't my family members treat me with more respect? Can't my family see how hard I work and how much I do for them?

But that's just the point. Those resentful questions reveal the condition of my heart. My Supermom thoughts are proof that I really don't care if I'm doing anything for my family at all.

Supermom embraces the spirit of entitlement. She operates on the wicked assumption that people owe her. People should worship her. People should be grateful to share the same house with her. People should *want* to serve her. She has a very high opinion of herself.

When Supermom's in charge, I'm keeping a clean house so that I can feel better about *me*. I'm more interested in achieving the satisfaction of personal accomplishment and even other's praise than in simply being faithful to my God and the ministry He has given me today inside my house, with my family, or at my job. I am primarily interested in Robin and being good at what I do, not in ministering to my family. Supermom thoughts are always selfish and full of pride. They are always sinful.

I'm convicted again by a line from missionary Amy Carmichael's poem "If."

> If I love to be loved more than to love,
> to be served more than to serve,
> then I know nothing of Calvary love.[2]

Ouch. How much do I really know about God's love for me?

If I know that I am in God's will, but I have a spirit of discontent and begin to feel that I deserve better than the position in which I currently find myself, Supermom is waving her victory banner over me. No growth in Christlikeness happens in a heart of discontent that is full of pride.

If I fulfill my duties as a mom and housewife, but expect some positive reinforcement from those I am serving, I'm not loving them at all. I'm just showing everyone how much I love myself.

I was recently slapped in the heart by this statement I've heard at different times in my life:

> I will most surely discover whether or not I have the servant-
> heart of Jesus when I'm treated like one.

I've found that the only way to get my heart back on the right track is to humble myself, confess my pride to God, and ask for His forgiveness. When I ask Him to take control of my spirit and teach me to be selfless, the burden of selfishness is lifted from me, and my heart is again full of joy in the Lord—even when I must sniff dirty laundry. I'm serious. I won't lie to you. I still don't like sniffing laundry, but at least my joy is not affected by it.

And it's a really, really good thing that true *joy* is never affected by our circumstances.

Once when I was under the kitchen table scraping dried carrots from the floor, I selfishly petitioned the Lord again for some kind of purpose in the menial tasks of housewifing, and His Spirit gently and humorously reminded me that since I hadn't spent enough time on my knees that morning, He was just giving me another opportunity to kneel before Him and commune with Him alone. Talk about a change of vision. Now when I see dried food on the floor under that table, I know that God loves me enough to have sovereignly planned yet another "date" with Him that day.

When we let Supermom take control of our motives, we only hurt ourselves and our loved ones. When loving God is our motive, we see His love for us in the way He sovereignly directs the smallest details of our existence—even under the kitchen table.

WHAT ABOUT ME?

1. Remembering Amy Carmichael's poem, do I love to be loved more than loving? Do I love to be served more than serving? If so, what do I really know of the love of God pouring out Himself for me on the bloody cross? Let the Spirit lay open your heart for examination as you carefully and fully answer these questions.

2. Thoughtfully consider the evidences of a person who is a glory thief. In which of these areas have you been tempted? In which have you failed? In which have you seen God's Word bring you victory?

3. Look at your list of circumstances and situations that your Supermom uses to tempt you to react selfishly. You know these situations will most likely reoccur. Write out and memorize a few battle plan verses to use the next time she attacks you in these areas.

4. How is the spirit of entitlement an evidence of deep-rooted selfishness?

O to be saved from myself, dear Lord,
O to be lost in Thee,
O that it may be no more I, dear Lord,
But Christ, that lives in me.[1]

A. A. Fitzgerald
Whiddington

Chapter Seven
The Battle of Blind Spots

In C. S. Lewis's *Screwtape Letters*, Wormwood's demon uncle offers his nephew advice on how to tempt the Christian he's been assigned to torment. Screwtape encourages Wormwood to offer the Christian man the delusion of neglecting the weakness within himself he doesn't want to acknowledge.

> You must bring him to a condition in which he can practice self-examination for an hour without discovering any of those facts about himself which are perfectly clear to anyone who has ever lived in the same house with him or worked in the same office.[2]

Supermom has said the same to me. Apparently she's a distant relative to Screwtape. She has persuaded me to take comfort in my blind spots, those areas of my heart that I just don't see clearly. You know, those things about me that are just part of who I am, part of who I've always been, and, if Supermom has her way, part of who I'll always be.

Supermom loves my blind spots. They are religiously acceptable excuses she can absolutely depend on. Especially since a *blind spot* is such a comfortable phrase in our postmodern Christian language. Don't we all just have things about ourselves that we may not be proud of? But hey, we all have weaknesses. It's just part of being human, right? Great spiritual pride is taken by those who just learn to overlook the faults of others without lovingly and humbly confronting the sin in their sisters' hearts.

When I asked God to begin showing me secret places in my heart I needed to deal with, I must say I was a bit irritated when He took me to my blind spots. Those are the weaknesses that are acceptable, excusable. I mean, I can't be perfect, right?

After getting near enough to see a number of my blind spots close up and personal, I began to realize something else. Most of my blind spots were negative in nature. They were some unflattering and ungodly parts of me. I also realized over time that technically they were areas that I wasn't actually blinded to. I knew they were there before I got close enough to see them in all their ugly glory. I discovered I was just really, really talented at ignoring them—that is until some hot water got poured on them and they reared their tacky heads to complain about it.

I also sadly discovered that my blind spots are areas that force my husband and children to grow in their sanctification. How pitiful is that? My blind spots are the thorns in my family's life. My blind spots are qualities about me my family has to put up with and pray about so that they respond lovingly. My blind spots don't naturally endear me to them. They can actually drive them away, and they are the reasons my husband and children must *choose* to love me. And frankly, loving me like they do is a full-time job.

My blind spots are areas where I'm teaching my children it's okay to excuse sin. They are watching me model respectable, excusable sins for them. Supermom loves these rooms of my heart house. She loves to see me tolerate the areas that I refuse to fully acknowledge.

I also found out that at some point in my life, I'd already been confronted with most of my blind spots, but because they were so painful, so personal, and required so much humility to deal with, I had just shoved them back into the corner and pretended not to see them. Then, because I love organizing and labeling things, I had slapped a big *Blind Spot* sticker on them and excused their presence in my life without a second glance. And there they sat, rotting away in my heart, having far-reaching sinful effects on my husband and children, and the body of Christ.

I can't even begin to count the number of times God has used some person or circumstance to move me into a situation to deal directly with one of my carefully labeled blind spots.

Take my anger, for example. You saw it in the battle with my pride, but I need to drag it out again. It touched so many days of my early momhood. Remember that it was tucked away in a secluded corner of my heart so long that I didn't even realize it was still there until I had toddlers and their antics shined a big beacon of light on that dusty old blind spot for me. Turned out I wasn't blind to it at all. I was very skillful at being mad.

Or take the time I was painting my daughter's room. Bobby had been out of town for almost two weeks at the time. I was tired in soul, spirit, and body, but I was determined to get pink stripes on one wall of her room before she turned three. I blocked my children safely out of the painting area, but my youngest son is the curious sort and was a very careful observer of all my actions, offering lively commentary along the way. When nature called, I carefully closed the paint can, put the brush high on a shelf out of temptation's way. I issued a clear command for the curious bystanders to refrain from entering the construction zone, and then I escaped to the bathroom for the one-minute marathon "break" all mothers of young children are personally familiar with.

About twenty seconds before my minute of privacy was up, I heard my three-year-old saying worriedly, "No, twins, no, no, no!" My heart sank. I rushed to cut my break short.

Five seconds before I opened the door, I heard the pattering of six little feet, some distant patting of little hands on the wall, some giggling and squealing.

As I turned the handle on the bathroom door, they heard me, and they panicked. "Mommy's coming!" they screamed. There was the sound of madly rushing bodies pumped full of adrenaline as they tried not to get caught.

As I came around the corner of the hall, I saw three little bodies disappearing into the other bathroom. And then I became aware that through the kitchen and dining room, down the hall, and into the bedroom were little footprints of wet white paint on the tan linoleum floor. In the next second I observed little handprints of wet white paint decorating the mustard yellow hall walls. And in the third second, I saw my little angels hurriedly wiping their paint-covered hands and feet on their beautiful monogrammed primary-colored towels, a gift from their grandmother at Christmas a month before.

And I lost it. Supermom took over in all her glory, waving her weapon of anger in my children's faces. I yelled at them and unleashed the fury in my heart. That evil Supermom in me used my words to hurt them, demean them, and make them feel thoroughly debased and unloved.

After about five minutes of my tirade, I realized they were all frozen in time, staring at me as if I were a crazed lunatic, as if I clearly was the one with the problem in this situation.

I remember I put their little paint-covered bodies in the empty bathtub, sat on the bathroom floor, and wept. I cried because I was mad. I cried because I was tired. I cried because they had just created hours of more work for me, because they had ruined the walls and floors in several rooms as well as the new towels, because in spite of my precautions they had still gotten into the paint! I cried because Bobby wasn't home, because I was alone, because I was trying so hard to be a good mom, but clearly wasn't succeeding, because I had lost my temper again and felt guilty about it, and because surely I deserved better than this.

I called Bobby some time in that first half hour and told him what had happened. I told him exactly what I thought of it all too, while the kids sat staring at me from the bathtub, listening to every word. No wonder that poor man didn't enjoy our phone conversations back then. I usually called him when I needed to dump emotionally. He probably cringed every time he saw my name pop up on his cell phone.

I remember my three toddlers just looking at me, not daring to move, knowing they were in *big* trouble. But what I remember most was the sadness in my three-year-old's eyes.

We just sat there for a good thirty minutes and looked at each other as I tried to calm down and the paint dried into the carpet and towels. Then Cotter in his toddler sweetness put me to shame.

"We sorry, Mommy," he whispered.

In that moment I was completely humbled. My toddler had apologized first. I was the one that was supposed to be the mature Christian adult who walked in the Spirit, who showed my little ones the love of Jesus. And I had just screamed, ranted, and displayed all the aspects of a really good temper tantrum. In my anger, I had just acted like a toddler.

I was the one that should have apologized first. I should have been the model of conflict resolution, of unconditional love, and of patience. But I was so mad, and I wanted to stay mad at my children, at my husband, and at God. I didn't want to forgive any of them for doing this to me.

That's when God showed me the real, hateful, sinful anger in my heart. The anger that was always there, that I had seen faintly at other times in my life, but that I had never dealt with. And that's when He used my children to break me and to force me to deal with this blind spot that I hadn't really ever actually acknowledged. He showed me what I really was: a self-centered woman who was willing to lash out in anger to hurt those around her when she didn't get what she wanted.

I remember I cried some more. This time sobs of sorrow. My children watched me intently from the tub, dried paint in their hair and new pajamas, unsure of their fate. I remember praying out loud to God, confessing my anger and begging for His help to love my children no matter what they did and to love them the way that He loved me.

So, with God's help, I apologized to my toddlers for my sinful anger. I told them I was wrong to yell at them like that, to not have self-control, and to be hateful to them with my words.

I asked them if they would forgive me. And to my shame, their forgiveness was immediate, full, and sweet. There was no holding grudges for them.

"Es, Mommy! I porgive!" Cotter said cheerfully. The twins nodded at me, their eyes still wide and clothes now stiff with dried paint.

I helped them apologize to me for their disobedience and for causing total destruction in the house. They received firm and appropriate punishment for their disobedience. And I forgave them. Sweet forgiveness. It was the antithesis of Supermom and the beginning of restoration.

Later, I asked two-year old Caeden, who had dipped his little feet into the paint can and run down the hall, how he got into the can in the first place. "With the 'driver, Mommy, yike you!" That little man had watched me carefully pry open the paint can with a screwdriver. He was watching me closely as I did what I did, and then he turned around and copied me. What a completely scary thought!

Caeleigh, not to be outdone, had dipped her little hands into the paint and decorated the wall with handprints. Cotter was alarmed at first, but what three-year-old wouldn't join in the fun? Not wanting to get paint on his hands, he had climbed up to retrieve the paintbrush, dipped it deep into the can, and flung it all over the bedroom, giving the bedding, furniture, and walls a bespeckled, splattered effect.

It took hours of cleanup. I had plenty of time to look closely at the anger in my heart, call it what it was, and confess it. No more excusing it by pretending to be blind to it—pretending it wasn't there.

Supermom wanted me to see my anger as a rightful weapon of choice for a tired, put-upon mother, like I deserved to get the emotional release of blowing up when something went wrong. She wanted me to use it to threaten my children into submission and to cause them to cower in fear of me, rather than in love for God. She deceived me into being self-focused, rather than acting like a forgiven child of God. She wanted me to feel sorry for myself and to make others pay for how they wronged me, and I fell for it. Yes, anger was a good weapon in her arsenal, and she wanted me to learn to use it well, even if I didn't use it very often.

CHOOSING TO SEE

God says the process of sanctification—of becoming more like Jesus—is His choice for me. He takes me by the hand and leads me to those areas of sin in my heart I want to avoid. He leads me so He can restore my soul by forcing me to turn and look at my sin and make a decision about what to do with it. He doesn't just let me slide. He presents me with choices every day—obey God or give in to Supermom.

Typically a blind spot is a spot or area we can't see at a quick glance into our mirrors. It's that little area to the back of the driver in a vehicle between her rearview mirror and her side mirror, that spot shielded from the field of vision visible in her mirrors.

Experienced drivers know it's there and that prudence says to turn your head and check your blind spot before merging into that lane. Every good driver's education instructor teaches his students to check their blind spots before merging. Every good driver makes it a habit.

But the blind spot really isn't a blind spot when you take the time to physically turn and look at it. You can see clearly a vehicle in that space then, maybe not the entire vehicle, but enough of it to know it's there. It's only a blind spot when you're depending on your mirrors to be accurate. When you use your God-given eyes and turn your body to look, you can see what's there just fine.

Can it be that my blind spots are likewise areas of unchecked or unchallenged sin? Have I become so accustomed to habits and personality traits being a part of who I am that I no longer see them as an enemy, but a permanent fixture in my soul? Have I excused some sin in my life for so long that I see it as an immoveable part of me like a lamp on an end table that I dust and arrange? Do I even sigh sometimes and wish for a better lamp but never actually get close enough to toss out the old one and replace it with a new one?

Do I recognize that my personality trait, that comfortable old part of me that everyone around me has just had to come to accept, is actually a sinful old pet habit that I'm just too lazy, too selfish to toss out and replace?

This could be my impatience with people who don't get things done as quickly as I'd like them to, or my unloving spirit towards people who talk too much and listen too little. This could be my laziness when I decide in my impatience to just do something myself rather than take the time to actually instruct my children in how to accomplish it. Do you know how many times I've tried to teach them to put their dirty clothes in the laundry? Oh, wait. You do know. You're doing the same thing with your children.

But blind spots, well, I must say I like them. If I'm *blind* to something, then technically I'm *not accountable* for it either. It wouldn't be fair to hold me accountable for something I can't even see. Supermom graciously accepts and excuses my sinful weaknesses, even while she judges others for theirs.

And if I can't see a blind spot—a spot that I *am* actually blind to—will God hold me accountable for it? Can I say to God in heaven when He points out my impatient spirit, "Wow! How did that get there? Where did that come from? I'm so glad you're not going to hold me accountable for *that* sin! I labeled it *Blind Spot* because I just didn't want to deal with it, so I'm not actually accountable for it, you see."

Nope. I just don't see that going over well with my loving heavenly Father.

I know that if I depend only on mirrors while I'm driving, I'm not a safe driver. I'm actually a pretty foolish one. When I nail the car next to me because I checked only my mirrors but didn't check my blind spot, you can be sure the police officer won't take that as an excuse. He's not going to say, "Poor over-worked mom, you were just too tired to turn around and check your blind spot. I won't give you a ticket this time." If you're driving the car, you're accountable for what you damage with it. And I can count on a ticket if I hit another car, even if it was in my blind spot.

I'm discovering that if I depend on only the mirrors in my heart, I don't see my sin clearly either. I'm being foolish, and we all know what the Bible says about fools.

> A foolish woman is clamorous: she is simple, and knoweth nothing. (Proverbs 9:13)

> The way of a **fool** is right in his own eyes: but he that hearkeneth unto counsel is wise. (Proverbs 12:15)

> Every wise woman buildeth her house: but the **fool**ish plucketh it down with her hands. (Proverbs 14:1)

> As a dog returneth to his vomit, so a **fool** returneth to his folly. (Proverbs 26:11)

> He that trusteth in his own heart is a **fool**: but whoso walketh wisely, he shall be delivered. (Proverbs 28:26)

I'm without excuse though. Being lazy spiritually doesn't excuse me from the damage done or the penalty incurred because I didn't check my blind spot.

Once when I was driving home from a ladies' missions tea, I had all three children with me. They had missed their afternoon nap so mommy could have some girl time and pray and eat cookies with her friends. The twins were screaming from their car seats. Cotter decided as I pulled into the driveway to disobey. I hit the garage door opener, slammed on my brakes at the entrance to the garage, and dealt with him.

Then, still correcting Cotter who had added his tired wails to the cacophony from the backseat, I began to inch into the garage. I heard the most awful, grating, screeching sound. Even the kids stopped screaming in shock. Slamming on my breaks again,

I put the van into park and opened the door to see what had happened. My guess is that the garage door hadn't fully opened, and when I inched into the garage, the door had caught on the luggage rack on top of the van. As I continued my forward motion, the garage door had been yanked off its runners and had folded backwards on top of my van.

My first thought was my husband and his reaction when he found out about this. My second thought was that I needed to fix this before he got home. The kids started screaming again.

I could tell that if I simply backed out of the garage, the dangling garage door would crash into my windshield, in all likelihood cracking it. Not good. I had to somehow back the van out of the garage without letting the garage door fall onto the windshield. So I opened my van door, and with one foot on the brake and one foot hopping backwards on the ground and with one hand on the steering wheel and one hand outside the car extended upwards to catch the falling garage door, I began to inch back out of the garage.

My plan worked. I was able to catch the dangling garage door after it unhooked from the luggage rack before it hit the windshield. But while I was hopping backwards on one foot, I didn't notice my proximity to the side of the garage, or the fact that my van door was going to hit it. Not just hit it, but bend completely backward as I continued my crazed hopping and looking up at the dangling garage door. In protecting my windshield, I had bent my van door to a rakish angle.

Picture that. I'm standing there half in and half out of the van holding the suspended garage door in my hands to the tune of three screaming toddlers. I was stunned. I decided to focus on my children first. I remember that one at a time I got my toddlers out of their car seats and put them down for their naps. Then I went out and surveyed the damage.

The garage door hung free of the runners. The runners were bent and mangled. The van door was bent backwards and couldn't be bent back to shut.

I couldn't bear the thought of telling Bobby, so I called my dad, who was three states away. He was sympathetic. I think he tried hard not to laugh. He did tell me to call my insurance company and get answers before calling Bobby, since men like to see their wives take initiative to fix the messes they create. He assured me that Bobby would still love me.

So I did all of that, and I used a sledgehammer to get the garage door back on its runners. It wobbled and screeched loudly when it was opened, but at least it worked. Mostly.

But there was nothing I could do about that van door. If I had just chosen to turn around and anticipate the trouble the blind spot behind me would cause, I could have prevented a whole lot of heartache. And just because I didn't see my van door getting ready to crash into the wall, I wasn't relieved of the consequences of it.

My dad was right. My husband still loved me, but I haven't been to another ladies' missions tea in years. I'm not sure we can afford it.

MIRRORS

So what mirrors in my heart do I use that actually contribute to protecting my blind spots? What mirrors leave a convenient space of gray "blindness" so that I do not see my sinful heart clearly?

When I asked God and my husband this question, they were both glad to help compile my list. Well, my husband was a bit hesitant at first. It seems that he's been burned before by his angry wife. *Sigh*. And yes, it was painful to set aside my excuses and deal with these issues. Supermom likes rotten junk in my heart. She's out to destroy me, remember?

Here's a list of the mirrors I discovered I prefer to consult rather than purposefully looking at my sin and dealing with it.

Personality

For me one of those mirrors is my personality. I excuse a whole lot of personal sins when I look at them through the lens of my personality.

"That's just the way you are," Supermom whispers. "God made you that way. You just tend to get things done quickly. It's just too bad everyone else can't move as quickly as you can. And," she reasons, "since that's just the way you are, you don't really need to apologize for your impatient spirit. Your family knows you are like that, and they'll get over it."

What about my lack of compassion? That's part of my personality too. I'm just not a people pleaser, and I don't feel compelled to have my emotional needs met by other people. I'm a homebody, and frankly, other people's emotional needs wear me out. Supermom quickly offers a spiritual-sounding rationalization. "Aren't you glad you're not so dependent on other people like that?"

She doesn't want me to love like Jesus does, so she graciously excuses my impatience when others slow me down. "After all," she whispers, "You are such a productive person. You probably should pray for that other person to become more productive like you are." Supermom doesn't want me to deal with my pride in skills that were given to me by God. She wants me to be a glory thief. Remember?

She also helps me justify my lack of love for others. "People are just exhausting, and too much interaction will keep you from getting things done," she reasons. And while for some that may be true in an extreme case, for me, it's a really good excuse to avoid loving others in practical ways.

I tend to be an introspective person. That in itself is not a sin, but when I excuse un-Christlike behavior in myself based on my personality style, it most certainly becomes a big ugly sin.

Background

Another favorite mirror is my background mirror. My conscience was dramatically shaped and influenced in my growing-up years. I was blessed with two Christian parents who loved me unconditionally, who sacrificed their personal comfort to put me in a solid Christian school, and who helped me attend a Christian university. Many experiences in my background directly influence the way I think and interact with others today. Your background affects you too.

What's appropriate to wear? What music is edifying? What expectations do I have of my husband? How often do we really need to go to church? What is my role in our home? What's my first response when someone wrongs me? How do I treat people of another race? How do I manage my finances? What impact do historical events in our nation have on my view of God? The answers to these questions are greatly shaped by my background, and Supermom uses that to her advantage. "That's just the way you were raised," she counters.

I usually check my background mirror when I'm getting ready to be critical of someone. "How inappropriate! Doesn't she know better than to wear that to church of all places? Can you believe anyone would have that sort of disrespect?" exclaims Supermom in my heart. Or she reminds me that "every husband should help his wife with the dinner dishes and take out the trash. After all, that's what *your* dad did." Supermom loves to use my background mirror to set me up for disappointment by making others appear as failures in my life when compared to my background. As if everyone else should think the way I think and act the way I do because of how my conscience was shaped by my background. So rather than turn and actually consider the issue from God's point of view, I simply check my background mirrors, make a judgment call, and move on, satisfied in my critical spirit toward others.

This works the opposite way too. What about relationships in my past that have been painful? Trusts that I have had broken? Circumstances and people who have genuinely broken my heart? Can I use those past hurts and my feelings from those situations to color my relationships in the present? Just because one person hurt me in the past, am I justified by that painful past experience to close up my heart to loving and being vulnerable to people in my present or in my future? Supermom screams, "Yes! You're the victim. Don't be the victim again. Protect yourself. People are not to be trusted, and you certainly can't love the ones who have hurt you in the past." Supermom loves to hold up my background mirror for me to carefully replay those painful circumstances when I'm trying to make decisions about relationships in the present.

Character

If I'm feeling really spiritual, I'll look into my character mirror. This mirror shows me real issues I should address, but allows me to ignore the root cause of those issues. Supermom loves this one because she knows it satisfies my conscience.

I look into my character mirror and see what I want to believe is just a minor weakness. I've found Supermom blinds me to my sinfulness best when I compare myself to other women around me. As it turns out, from Supermom's point of view, most everyone else's weaknesses are worse than mine. But, she counters from her lofty pedestal of pride, you want to be able to relate to them. So, she helps me to find someone that does something better than I do. She helps me compare. Then I feel the appropriate amount of Supermom guilt. She helps me decide I just need to work harder to be better at doing more.

For example, I see that I have a weakness in showing mercy in my character mirror because the sister in the pew next to me takes more food to the sick people in our church than I do, so I give another prayer request at the Wednesday night prayer meeting. "Please pray that I'll take more initiative in meeting the needs of those around me," I humbly confess. I've now confessed in false public humility a weakness to others, but I missed altogether the fact that the real problem is my sinful selfishness. What a prideful reprobate I am. What I should have been doing was confessing my horrible selfishness to those dear sisters and my lack of love for others. The reason I wasn't "taking initiative in showing compassion" was because I didn't have any real compassion in my heart in the first place. I wasn't loving others the way Christ loves me.

But Supermom wants me to focus on my surface issues, so rather than deal with the root pride in my heart, she'd rather I focus on becoming a better person in my quest to be all that Supermom should be. She's out to look good. She knows that if I can just keep myself busy in changing a character flaw, she can get me to avoid the bigger sin issue in my heart.

Expectations

Expectations are such powerful tools in the hands of Supermom. I struggle with this one so much that I've already written an entire chapter of this book—chapter five—to deal with it. But I'll look at expectations again in this chapter.

What do I expect from others? What do they expect from me? What do I expect from myself? Expectations can also be what I consider my personal rights, and my expectations mirror is very helpful in avoiding a close look directly at my heart motives.

The Supermom in me expects that our house should remain in a mostly clean and organized state, and when I put the personal effort into keeping it clean, I earn certain rights to its clean state. Woe to the individual who messes with this expectation.

If I get impatient and unloving to my husband and children when they tramp dirt into the house, leave rotten apple cores in the family room or muddy fingerprints on the back door, Supermom says that's okay. The end totally justifies the means. The expectation of a clean house is more important to Supermom than loving like Jesus did.

"So jump down their throats when they're lazy. They deserve it," affirms Supermom. "Focus on your expectations and train everyone else to give you what you want," she encourages. She works to convince me that I deserve a certain reality, as well as people in my life who give me the reality I want.

Using my expectation mirror, she sets everyone around me up for failure in my eyes and generously gives me free rein to express my feelings of disappointment in them for their lack of success in meeting my expectations. No one is really ever good enough for Supermom. She looks down from her lofty position of pride and is generally displeased with the people in her world.

Insecurities

This is a frequently used mirror in my life that my dear husband pointed out to me. It has far-reaching effects I'm just beginning to understand. I tend to be a very insecure person. My insecurity manifests itself in a variety of ways.

Supermom tells me this is okay. She reminds me that I'm a woman, and most women tend to deal with some insecurities about something. While statistically this is probably true, it's not an excuse for allowing it to abide in my heart.

I'm insecure about who I am, about my abilities, about what I look like, about whether or not Bobby loves me, about whether or not people I respect also respect me, about how my children reflect on me as their mother, and about if I'll even have a shred of dignity left at my church and with my friends after they've read this book revealing my sinful heart.

Supermom helps me look at my insecurity mirror and shift into blame gear easily. She offers multiple excuses to choose from. One of my favorite excuses has to do with the pounds on the scale. "You gave birth to three children—large children, I might add—before your third anniversary," she reminds me. "And you were in your thirties when you did so. Everyone knows the older you get, the harder it is to lose weight. You live in the woods buried in snow for five months out of the year. How are you supposed to get outside to exercise? You need to keep an extra layer of fat on yourself just to stay warm up here. Your husband travels. You're just too busy compensating for his absence and keeping up the house to exercise regularly. You have three toddlers, and every mom of toddlers deserves a bit of chocolate now and then." She then mentally plays the Dove chocolate commercial with its soothing music in my head, and I am fully justified.

On she goes as she skillfully helps me excuse myself for eating too much and not exercising enough. She did this for so long that I became very unhealthy, had no energy to keep up with my children, and avoided most social contact because of my dress size. This was her plan all along. She hates me. She wants to destroy me.

A few years ago, I was forced to deal with my unhealthy state at the doctor's office. Every number was out of whack, and it was my own fault. I began exercising, watching what I ate, and drinking more water. Within a year all of my numbers—cholesterol, blood sugar, triglycerides, and blood pressure—returned to normal. Every number changed except for the numbers on the scale. They did come down some, but they didn't return to their pre-baby spot. Not even close.

I was furious. I was doing everything right now, so why didn't I get rewarded for it? I had more energy and was sleeping well. I was strong again. My doctor said I was healthy, but still overweight. What's up with that? I wanted to be skinny again. I felt betrayed and discouraged.

And that's when God showed me how much I wanted the praise of people. I should have been focused on being a healthy individual so that I could be the woman, the wife, and the mother God created me to be. But when I was finally medically healthy again, I wasn't satisfied. I wasn't satisfied because the way other people viewed me was *way* too important to me. And even deeper in my heart, I discovered how I viewed *myself* was also *way* too important to me. Supermom accused me, berated me for not measuring up to her standards of perfection.

I was struck again at how I'd been deceived by Supermom. I had fallen for the secular idea that having a beautiful body was a key factor to my happiness. It's not, plain and simple. God expects me to exercise self-discipline, to avoid gluttony, and to keep my body in such a state of health that it's able to fulfill His expectations of me. But nowhere in the Bible do I see Him give me size specifications. Supermom sure does. She tells me exactly what I should look like and how much I must weigh before I can be a useful vessel for God. I allowed her to hold me back from ministry opportunities for years because I didn't meet her expectations.

And I'll be transparent with you, I still struggle with this. When I allow Supermom to turn my focus on myself, instead of focusing on how I can serve God and others, I struggle. My pride hurts. She even uses spiritual language to convince me of the futility of ministry if I don't look good by society's standards. She whispers, "Doesn't God deserve a beautiful vessel? Look at you. You're nowhere close. Better to keep your head down and lay low until you look good. God deserves better than you. You'd probably distract people from Him instead of glorifying Him." Oh, she's good at discouraging me and feeding the fire of my insecurities.

And then there's the other extreme. Sometimes she tempts me to hide my insecurity by overcompensating for it. "Be overly confident," she whispers, knowing full well that this misplaced confidence is in myself. "Just push forward, work hard, and minister," she demands. She uses guilt and manipulation to motivate me, so I depend on my God-given talents and skills rather than my God. And she's thrilled at my ineffectiveness, and I'm once again exhausted in my attempt to live the Christian life in my own ability.

God's showing me that my mirrors of insecurity mask my real problem, which is that I don't understand fully my secure position in Christ. Romans 8:14–17 assures me that "as many as are led by the Spirit of God, they are the sons of God. For ye have not received the spirit of bondage again to fear; but ye have received the Spirit of adoption, whereby we cry, Abba, Father. The Spirit itself beareth witness with our spirit, that we are the children of God: And if children, then heirs; heirs of God, and joint-heirs with Christ."

Because of the sacrifice of Jesus on the cross for me, I am now a child of God, a child with special privileges, an heir.

Remember that Supermom uses Satan's tactics, the same Satan that tempted Jesus after he had been fasting for forty days in the wilderness. Jesus was very, very hungry and the devil's first attempt to get Him to fall had to do with food. Clever, huh? But it's the way the devil posed his first question to Jesus that catches my eye. He used his word choice to plant the thought in Jesus' mind that His standing with God was on shaky ground. Satan says, "If thou be the Son of God, command this stone that it be made bread" (Luke 4:3).

What? *If*? *If* Jesus is the Son of God? Of course He's the Son of God! But the devil wanted Jesus to feel disconnected with His Father and from His Father's plan for His human life. Sound familiar?

Supermom attacks our position in Christ before God too. She makes us doubt our standing as His precious daughter. By her choice of words whispered in our minds, she creates a hesitation and uncertainty within our hearts.

Are you really God's child? You have a sin problem. Do you really think God loves you?

If that old devil who walks around like a roaring lion seeking everyone he can destroy (1 Peter 5:8) tried to get our Savior to doubt His position with God, then we can be sure Supermom will try the same trick on us.

And when I don't understand God's great love for me, then I look to others to meet my need for security. This is a need only my Creator can fill.

SEEING MYSELF

When I'm driving, mirrors can be helpful, but at best they offer a distorted view of reality. Looking at my heart through mirrors is definitely more comfortable, less invasive, and allows for more latitude in seeing what's really there. Mirrors leave room for excuses. And depending on how warped our mirror is, what we actually see can take on grossly misleading proportions. Remember the distorted mirrors that make you look extremely tall or extremely fat? (I, of course, always choose to stand in front of the one that makes me look skinny.)

But the only way to deal with the sin in my heart is to see it with the eyes of God revealed in His Word. As His hand leads me, I must look closely at the lamp on the end table that's been there since I can remember it. I don't get to turn sideways and view it through a mirror from a distance. He forces me to look at it directly, head on, and call it sin. That negative personality trait? Sin. That way of thinking I excused in myself from childhood? Sin. That weak character attribute I just wanted to work harder at attaining? Hiding a root sin that's become a fixture in my heart?

No, there aren't blind spots in my heart. There's just unconfessed, unacknowledged, unconfronted sin that's become comfortable and habitual. There's just sin that's been allowed to be part of me for so long, it's become something of a guest in my house.

I must deal with them. And you must deal with yours.

Bobby and I still have those paint-covered towels. We use them for our dogs. The paint-drenched carpet has been replaced with a laminate floor. I sanded most of the little handprints off the wall when I repainted, but if you stand sideways and catch the light just right by my bedroom door, you can see the faint outline of two little handprints underneath the fresh coat of paint. I left them as my reminders of the day God forced me to rip the *Blind Spot* label off, deal with my anger, and get the victory over Supermom.

The ripping part is painful, but refusing to mislabel our sin allows us to see anew God's love for us. And I'm finding it is well worth the pain.

WHAT ABOUT ME?

1. Do you believe God will hold you accountable for the sinful habits you've grown accustomed to excusing in your life?

2. Make a list of blind spots in your life. Better yet, ask a close, trusted friend or your husband to help you compile a more accurate list. Some good leading questions

might be, "How do I make it hard for you to love me?" or "I know I have habits or character issues that are frustrating to you. Would you mind sharing those with me?" Give them time to think about how to respond. Remember to be ready to receive with humility their answers.

3. Look at your blind spot list. What "mirrors" has Supermom used to help you mentally justify, rationalize, or excuse that sin in your life?

4. Systematically work through your list with God, recognizing your sin, its effects on others, and its devastating consequences. Then memorize verses to resist your sinful nature when you are tempted to excuse these sins in the future. Be sure to also reconcile the relationships that have been damaged by your blind spots in the past.

Through many dangers, toils and snares,
I have already come;
'Tis Grace hath brought me safe thus far,
And Grace will lead me home.[1]

John Newton

Chapter Eight
The Battle to Remember

The truth is, I like to remember the good stuff. It's just more fun! The pleasant memories; my precious friends; the hilarious encounters; the humorous events. I especially love dwelling on the mountaintop experiences that have shaped my journey. (Given the choice, I will choose a cool, crisp mountain vacation over a hot, sandy beach every time.) Mountaintop vistas are breathtakingly beautiful and easily memorable. But fruit is grown in the valleys.

And, frankly, as I take a quick journey down memory-lane, I am stopped cold at this reality: my deepest, most authentic personal growth to be like Jesus happens for me in the valleys of my life—in the hard times; in the lonely places; pressed under the pain of sorrow; against the jaggedness of uncertainty; through the brokenness of humility; at the end of myself.

Supermom loves the valleys. The hard times are her best opportunity to present me with the ripe fruit of bitterness. In my times of pain, she begs me to take and eat and let the roots drive deep into my soul. She wants me to enjoy its immediate, temporary sweetness and forget the juices that will first poison and then destroy me.

I'm finding it's in the valleys that God most often uses circumstances and people to reveal clearly to me who I really am.

Truthfully, in a time of conflict, I'd rather focus on the negative circumstances or frustrating children or anyone and anything else, including how to *fix* the situation to protect my reputation. But the Spirit marches me straight past the surface into the deeper pools of my reactions. It's not just about the situation. It's what He wants me to learn about my heart *in* the situation. He wants me to learn what He already knows about me.

These revealing situations sweep into our lives almost every day. God uses the kids' misbehavior in the store to reveal my unloving spirit and impatience. Do I excuse my behavior as a natural, acceptable response to someone else's sin? Or do I call my unloving spirit *sin*, run to the cross, confess my sin, and experience His forgiving grace?

God uses hurtful gossip of a supposed friend to reveal the anger in my heart. Do I excuse my carefully dropped comments of returned slander as a natural, acceptable response to someone else's sin? Or do I call my desire for retaliation *sin*, run to the cross, confess my sin, and experience His forgiving grace?

God uses a friend's promotion to reveal to me my jealousy. God uses a thief in my home to reveal to me my materialism. God uses a wayward child to reveal to me my desire to control, and a car accident to reveal my lack of eternal perspective. A disease diagnosis reveals a too-tight hold on this very temporary life.

Again, do I excuse these sins as a natural response? Or do I call each *sin*, run to the cross, confess my sin, and experience His forgiving grace?

Do you see that every time Supermom gets me to excuse my sin by mislabeling it, she robs me of the opportunity to run to the cross and experience His grace? She hates grace. She resents that you as a beloved child of God have access to it. She loves to offer a convenient mislabel for our sin so we can spiritually excuse it, and then we don't need His grace. And Supermom rejoices.

I must remember these battles against my sin and the reward of grace. If I don't remember, I'm prone to repeat the same sin pattern over and over again. What bondage! I'm saved by His grace! I must continue to live in it too.

CORRECTING MY VIEW

Jesus wants me to know and love His Father. Jesus suffered and died for the purpose of reconnecting His creation with His Father. He satisfied His Father's holiness so we could know His Father's love.

This beautiful, difficult, emptying-of-myself journey to become more like Jesus leads me to pursue His Father, to know God, to fervently study Him, His character, and His Words to me with the kind of passion David expresses in Psalm 42:1—to crave and pant for Him like a deer pants for clean water, because not to have Him is to *die*.

The more I see God, the more I stand in awe of His holiness. The more my spirit learns of His holiness, the more clearly I'm aware of my personal sinfulness. And the more I'm grieved by my sinfulness, the more I cry out with Isaiah, "Woe is me! for I am undone" (Isaiah 6:5).

I want to follow the footsteps of Paul whose own personal journey toward being like Jesus was perhaps most clearly evident in the changing way he viewed himself. Notice the downward spiral of his self-esteem:

- Toward the beginning of his ministry to the churches, he humbly says, "I am the least of the apostles, that am not meet to be called an apostle, because I persecuted the church of God" (1 Corinthians 15:9). Here he is comparing himself to the other apostles and believes he comes up on the lowest rung of these spiritual giants. There is the beginning of humility here in his self-assessment.

- Later during his first Roman imprisonment, Paul's view of himself has taken a downward turn. He refers to himself as I "who am less than the least of all saints"

(Ephesians 3:8). Now he's started comparing himself not to the apostles, but to all the other Christians around him and ranks himself as the lowest of them. Greater humility, perhaps, but his self-measuring stick hasn't reached far enough.

- At the end of his life, Paul writes to Timothy that "Christ Jesus came into the world to save sinners; of whom I am chief" (1 Timothy 1:15). His growing spiritual maturity continues to bring him to the foot of the cross of Jesus—to the gospel—where he now compares himself to the holiness of God and considers himself the greatest sinner in the world. This is authentic humility.

So how do I view myself?

Honestly, given free reign, my heart tends to think the best of me, to be first in my own cause, and to excuse and be gracious with me when I *struggle*. I don't really prefer to call my *struggles* by the ugly name *sin*. I mean, does a Christian girl simply have a *struggle* with impatience, or is her impatience truly a sin? Does she merely *indulge* in gossip, or is her gossip an actual nasty, evil separate-me-from-God kind of sin?

It's time we were honest with ourselves. Because truly, how you view yourself depends entirely on how well you know your God. The more you know Him, the less you think of yourself. The more you know Him, the more desperate you are for His grace. Because you are nothing, and He is indescribable.

UNEARNED LOVE AND UNDESERVED GRACE

I've fallen again and again and again for the eons-old deception of "doing right impresses God" trick the Pharisees embraced. I mean, it sounds so, well, *spiritual!* The first step on that slippery slope is usually made with very good biblical intentions: to please God.

Don't misunderstand! I'm not in any way saying it's wrong to want to please God! Paul says clearly when it comes to giving out the gospel: "even so we speak; not as pleasing men, but God, which trieth our hearts" (1 Thessalonians 2:4). Hebrews 11:5 talks about how Enoch escaped death because his faith pleased God. Verse six—the very next verse—tells us that it's impossible to please God unless we have faith.

James admonishes us that "faith without works is dead" in James 2:26. It's not wrong to want to do good works to please God. We should passionately be pouring out every part of our being to bring pleasure and glory to our amazing Father who has enabled us to be called His children. We owe Him everything. But His grace was never meant to be repaid. It was meant to be tasted, experienced, and savored.

Supermom loves to take truth and twist it . . . just a bit . . . so we will fall unsuspectingly into her self-reliant trap. Genuine faith in our redeeming God will naturally and rightly show itself in the way we live our lives, in the choices we make, and in the love we have for each other. (See James 2:17–20.)

But loving God changes *us*, not Him. It is wrong to think our doing things that please God somehow negates our sin issues, or somehow makes His grace unnecessary. Remember how the Pharisees of the Bible kept adding to what God had said, somehow thinking that doing more and more *good* would make them more and more acceptable to God? They were hoping that somehow, God would be impressed by those who work hard to be holy and would therefore love them more than He loves the wretched murderer caught in the bondage of sin and more than He loves the adulteress and more than the widow who could only give a mite.

But all my good works don't commend me to God—whether before or after my salvation from sin. Nothing I can do can make Him love me more than He already does.

> *But God commendeth his love toward us, in that,*
> *while we were yet sinners, Christ died for us.*
> *(Romans 5:8)*

My entire worth, identity, and value is found wholly in Jesus. Jesus purchased me. He paid the price for my sin and earned me the position before the throne of God as His child—His *beloved* child.

Spiritual maturity isn't becoming so perfect, so above reproach in my actions that I really have no need of the cross and grace of Jesus anymore. It's not a race to see who among us can impress God the most with our outward show of religiously-acceptable works. Good God-honoring works are what I do only because I'm His daughter and because I love Him.

At the end of time when all our good works are laid on the altar for God to evaluate, He says He will judge them by fire and then pass out crowns. (See 1 Corinthians 3:8–15, 9:24–25; 1 Thessalonians 2:19–20; James 1:12; Revelation 2:8–11; 2 Timothy 4:8; and 1 Peter 5:4.) God loves to bless His children and promises to reward them for what they did with their time on earth after their salvation. But good works alone are just not enough. They may trick others. But they can be a true "form of godliness" without being the real thing. (See 2 Timothy 3:5.)

Be painfully honest. Can any of our outward good actions that look like *godliness* be traced back to the selfish motive of impressing others, of looking like a good Christian girl, of conforming to an acceptable standard so that others—maybe even we ourselves—*think* we're good Christians, and so that we *feel* like good Christians?

True spirituality isn't equal with, or measured by, my performance. My performance is just an *effect*, not a *cause*. True spirituality goes much deeper than what I do. It's who I am. Real honest spiritual steps to be like Jesus mean I become more and more consumed by how desperately in need of the cross I really am, especially *after* becoming His child.

So should I knock myself out trying to have the right view of myself? No, not at all. Humility isn't something to acquire so I can check it off my "How to Please God" checklist. Humility is simply a beautiful result of having my eyes opened to the holiness of God. For when I really see Him, I see myself for who I am, the chief of sinners.

Sister, beg God to take you on this journey of knowing Him more deeply, more intimately. It's the journey of the deepest Love you will ever know.

THE TROUBLE WITH TRANSPARENCY

I'm a sinner. So are you. Not in some vague sense of "poor us, we have a little badness in us, don't we?" But in an "I'm capable of every single evil sin possible if it weren't for the grace of God" kind of way.

Why don't we like to remember this? Why aren't we comfortable with admitting this to ourselves? If we're not being honest with ourselves about the breadth of our sinfulness, we can't be honest with others either. Why is it our tendency to avoid true vulnerability with our sisters in Christ? Who do we think we're protecting? What means more to us: our precious public "testimony" or knowing God on a level that leaves us without any defense but the cross of Jesus and brings the natural fruit of humility and gratefulness?

What is transparency? Why does it matter?

I'm going to pull out the Webster's 1828 dictionary again for this one. Transparency is *that state or property of a body by which it allows rays of light to pass through it, so that objects can be distinctly seen through it.*

When we apply this principle of transparency to our Christian walk, it means that our lives are so truly clear and our hearts so free from any covering that His light shines forth from us. It means that nothing stands in the way of an outside observer seeing the truth of Christ shining through us.

Transparency is a powerful word. Being transparent doesn't mean that in communicating about the realities of my sin I glorify that sin in any way. It means I honestly portray how deep my need is for the transforming grace of God. Transparency with others isn't inviting sympathy or pity from them. It's laying bare my heart with no pretense, no prideful covering, and no deceitful façade so that everyone who sees into my life will be amazed at God's work in this heart. It isn't joking about or minimalizing a pet sin habit with my girlfriends. It's communicating my genuine grief when I give in to the sneaky, cunning temptations to sin that daily attack me.

Transparency is humiliating to Supermom. She finds it uncomfortable, unnecessary, and unprofitable. She prefers the seclusion and fictitious elevation of her pedestal. She doesn't want anyone to get a good look at the state of her heart. She doesn't want you to see the truth of its sinfulness. She doesn't want anyone to see her hungry need for the transformation only God's grace can bring to her. Pride cloaks her desperate state from her own eyes. Remember that pride blinded Lucifer too.

Transparency like this breeds a beautiful unity between us because it strips us of all pretense, social status, and expectation. It gathers us all on equal footing before the cross of Jesus, and at the cross we find that we are, after all, much the same—completely dependent on Him.

At the foot of the cross in humble recognition of our sin and need for Jesus is usually where the deepest friendships of our lives are born. Genuine transparency generates a level of connectivity with other Christians that is absolutely riveting and powerful in its results. Think about it. Most likely the meaningful friendships of your life were forged in some trial of adversity where genuine transparency became the norm, and it's in those friendships that we catch a brief glimpse of the sweet fellowship that awaits us in heaven.

Transparency transcends vague prayer requests, generalizations about sin, and polite conversations about things that don't really matter. It goes deeper, further, higher in to the amazing reality of James 5:16.

> *Confess your faults one to another, and pray one*
> *for another, that ye may be healed. The effectual*
> *fervent prayer of a righteous man availeth much.*

Isn't it interesting that healing is preceded by our prayers for one another and that the humility of transparency, confessing our faults to one another, precedes effectual prayer?

Notice James's straightforward instructions about what to do with those confessions: *pray* for each other. He doesn't tell us to judge, gossip, or act shocked at our sister's sin. We *know* her sin struggle, because it's our own. We all fight the very same battles. We all have the same Savior. We all carry the same weapon of power, and we all have each other.

I have no doubt that one of Supermom's greatest roadblocks to transparency is the fear of being vulnerable to other sinful women. Every one of us has been burned in the past by some form of slander or gossip. Probably at some point, every one of us has also been the one doing the burning.

Supermom wants to avoid being vulnerable. It's too scary. Being vulnerable means I have to see myself honestly. Seeing myself honestly requires that my understanding and intimate relationship with God is growing. Knowing God reveals to me an ever-increasing awareness of my sinful state—*my* sinful state. Not someone else's sin and not some vague corporate group sinfulness of general humanity. Mine. Understanding my desperate sinful state leads me to experience grace again and again. Supermom wants to avoid this at any cost.

REMEMBERING

God makes a big deal in Scripture about His people remembering His work that always followed their inadequacy. In fact He told them over and over in the Old Testament to *remember* Him! They were told to write things down, to build altars and erect stones all for the sake of remembering who God is, what God had done for them, and how they should trust Him in the future.

Take the Israelites crossing the Jordan River, for instance, in Joshua 3–4. Joshua was the brand new leader of the Israelites. God was leading them into the Promised Land, but many were fearful of the heathen nations that already lived in the land. And this raging, flood-stage river stood between them and God's promises, much like Supermom stands between us and victory.

God gave them clear instructions about how to cross. These Israelites had heard their parents talk about how God had parted the Red Sea and saved them from the Egyptians, but none of these people had actually experienced that, except for Joshua. Now it was time for them to experience God's deliverance for themselves. The priest actually had to march by faith with the ark of the covenant into the raging river, and then God stopped its flow, and the rest of the Israelites passed through it on dry ground. Wow! What a life-changing experience!

But God knows us, and He knew His people well. He knew their tendency to forget the devastating reality of the situation and the miraculous deliverance of their God. They'd forgotten before. I've forgotten before. So God told Joshua to set up two memorials of twelve stones—stones taken from the middle of the Jordan River—for two purposes: "that all the people of the earth might know the hand of the Lord, that it is mighty" and "that ye might fear the Lord your God for ever" (Joshua 4:24).

One memorial was set up on the side of the Jordan for all to see, and one memorial was set up right smack in the middle of the Jordan. It's now under water, but at the time the book of Joshua was written, the Bible says in Joshua 4:9 that "they are there unto this day."

Just like the Israelites, I can take stones from my present momhood battles and put them in a place where just God and I know about them, a place where I can go to remember who He is, who I am, and what He in His love has done for me. But I can also set them up where they can be seen by others to incite curiosity and to point others to my God.

The Israelites' stones were set up in a public place next to the river to prompt their children for generations to ask, "What mean these stones?" (See Joshua 4:21.) And whenever the children asked about those stones, their parents would look at that stack of rocks and remember that in their inability, their God was mighty to save and that they personally could trust Him forever. God didn't mean for the stones to remind them about how nice the weather was that day, what they wore, who they walked along with, or how exciting the adventure was. The stones were meant to remind them of their personal failure and the God-given victory, of their inadequacy to solve their problem, of God's power in every situation, of their decision to trust in Him, and of the awesome God that took their faith and moved the river for them.

That's what scars are—memory-bearers. Scars are the visible reminder of past pain. Even Jesus kept his scars in His resurrected body. Why? Scars help us to remember. They remind us of the real pain, real suffering, and real physical and spiritual battles He fought. They remind us that He won. It was Christ's scars that proved to Thomas in John 20:24–29 that this man was indeed the same Jesus whom Thomas had seen crucified a few days before. Scars were proof. Scars can be beautiful when they remind us of God's goodness.

My stones, my memories, my scars from momhood should be visible so that they remind me too, so that they keep me from memories that tend to be self-indulgent and imply my self-sufficiency, and so that they incite curiosity from my children about this God that gives victory. They should give my sisters in Christ hope as well. When I show you the real stones taken from the midst of my real battles with Supermom, they should point you straight to God, not to my stamina, not to unique circumstances, and not to the people involved. But to my weakness and God's power to change a sinful mom.

How I valued the godly veteran moms who cheered me on, took time to meet practical needs, and wrapped their arms around me in support. I praise God for faithful soldier-moms who have given biblical counsel, meals, laundry skills, and encouragement to show God's love to the newbies. We are eternally grateful!

Among these wise veterans are my own precious mother and dear mother-in-law who have given of themselves, their time, their prayers, and their love over and over again to bless me with hope. Another group of three friends and I met twice a year at night after all our babies were asleep to have coffee and pray with and encourage each other. It was literally the only time we tired mamas had to get together, and it was time well spent. Those friendships forged in the early fires of motherhood continue to this day, though we are now scattered across the world.

I have one friend, in particular, who is just ahead of me in the momhood trenches. She is a friend who knows God and is therefore painfully aware of her sinful bent. She humbly and openly shares her struggles—her stones—with me. This friend isn't a trained counselor or public speaker, and she doesn't ever seek the public spotlight. She's just a faithful, behind-the-scenes kind of Christian mom who daily battles her own Supermom. But she has taken the time to come alongside of me, to listen to my sin battles with an open heart, and then to lovingly confront me and encourage me in Christlikeness. And she asks me to do the same for her.

Friends like this are few and far between. This veteran mom's counsel is precious to me because it's biblical and it's real. She hasn't forgotten the early struggles with her Supermom because she set up her stones to remember. And because she hasn't forgotten her sin battles, she hasn't forgotten the One who gave her the victory.

I don't want to forget either. I want to set up as memorials these stones of remembrance just like the Israelites did by the Jordan River. I want to remember my battles with sin that God won. I want to remember the victory that comes when I step out by faith like the Israelites did into that raging Jordan River overflowing its banks in flood stage. Yes, I want to remember all the precious, fleeting moments I have with my babies, their unique smiles, their soft little heads, their precocious stumbling words as they learn to talk, and that amazing thrill that races through me when they slip their trusting hands into mine or snuggle in for a hug.

But I also want to remember my weakness, my struggles, and my broken state. These represent stones that I can't get to unless I step out in total trust of my perfect God. I want to remember so that I can give God the glory by being ready to give an answer to other moms about the hope that lies within me now. Because someday I know God will give me the opportunity to minister to a new mom, an exhausted, battle-weary, sinful mom like me. When she asks me about my first years as a mother, I want to show her empathy and compassion. But I don't want to present her merely with a Hallmark-card view of the spiritual momhood battlefield or leave out my struggles. I don't want to give in to the temptation to present myself in a better light or give a good impression of myself. I want her to see my stones carried out of the midst of my battles. I want to honestly share with her the glaring reality of my battle with sin. Because then, and only then, can I share with her the amazing grace, the overwhelming love, and the living power of my God. I can show her how His Sword, the Word of God, helped me defeat temptations, and point her to my God who alone has given me the victory.

It is one thing to read a historical war account in a book. It's quite another experience to hear an actual veteran share with you personally the sights, sounds, and heartbreak of a battle he survived.

So, quick! Before it's too late and our memory fades, let's take a thoughtful open-eyed trip into the recent past. Set up our stones. Write down the early sin battles we faced and the specific ways we have tried to be a Supermom and failed. Write down ways God gave us the victory over our sin, how He humbled us, encouraged us, strengthened and empowered us with His Word. In our weakness, He is strong. (See 2 Corinthians 12:9.)

Just to be clear, I'm not talking about allowing past sins to overwhelm you with guilt and fear again. In Philippians 3:13–14 Paul says "but *this* one thing I *do*, forgetting those things which are behind, and reaching forth unto those things which are before, I press toward the mark for the prize of the high calling of God in Christ Jesus." We should never allow the old sinful habits and past situations to bog us down. Those sins must be humbly confessed and forsaken, and we must move forward to claim the victory God wants to give to us!

But when you've been given amazing victory over sin by the grace of God, it's something worth remembering, worth singing about, and worth rejoicing over. Humbly acknowledging my past sins allows me to exalt God's victory in my life. Many of the greatest hymns were written by composers who were simply pouring out praise to a God who had saved them from a life of sin bondage. They remembered who they were, sinners without hope, and with grateful hearts they pointed people to the God of their salvation. Their testimonies of God's grace continue to point people straight to God. If you don't know any of these inspiring stories, start with the story behind *Amazing Grace*. It's beautiful! Paul also did this often in his letters by reminding those new Christians that they had once been in bondage to sin but now are free because of the grace of God. (See 1 Corinthians 6:9–11, Ephesians 2:19, Colossians 1:21–22, and Titus 3:3–7)

When we are no longer amateurs at momhood and our time comes to encourage the next recruits, we need to speak up. They need to hear about how God gave us the victory over our Supermoms and how God continues to give us victory. Our stones of remembrance can point them to Him.

No, new moms are not in any way dependent on us to find victory in His Word. But we should be faithfully encouraging them to fight to win their battles against the sin that so easily deceives us and then hardens our hearts. Consider this challenge from Hebrews 3:13:

> *But exhort one another daily, while it is called*
> *To day; lest any of you be hardened through the*
> *deceitfulness of sin.*

We can join with the author of Hebrews in speaking truth and encouragement to these new moms. See how he assumes our battle with sin and encourages us to persevere in the journey by looking to Jesus?

*Wherefore seeing we also are compassed about with
so great a cloud of witnesses, let us lay aside every
weight, and the sin which doth so easily beset us,
and let us run with patience the race that is set before us, looking unto Jesus the author and finisher
of our faith; who for the joy that was set before
him endured the cross, despising the shame, and is
set down at the right hand of the throne of God.
(Hebrews 12:1–2)*

This book is one of my stones. As you walk through your Jordan, as you stand on the other side and watch the waters flow again, remember. Set an actual stone up on your kitchen window sill to remind you. My beloved next-door neighbor uses a dry-erase marker to write her battle plan verses on her kitchen window regularly so that she will be reminded to keep her mind stayed on her God to be ready to fight her own Supermom.

I beg you to be ready. Your day to minister is coming. Your day to pass on the battle plan for victory will arrive, and when it does, share all your precious, chaotic, and fun memories of early momhood. But please don't stop there. Be humble. Remember with clarity. Be honest. Be transparently courageous and encourage that young mother in her personal battle with Supermom.

Remember she really doesn't need our nostalgia or our sense of humor. She needs God. Give her God, and you'll give her hope. Don't let her be merely a survivor. Help her become a victor. Help her run to grace.

WHAT ABOUT ME?

1. Have you ever felt disconnected from the shared experiences of a veteran mom? If so, the next time memories are being shared by a trusted veteran, have your questions ready to dive deeper. Ask her:
"For you, what was the most difficult part of being a new mom?"
"What did you learn most about God during your first

years as a mother?"

"What verses did God use to encourage you most?"

"Did you ever feel like a failure?"

"What suggestions do you have for me as I fight my sin nature?"

These kinds of questions will take the conversation to beautiful new depths, connecting your spirits as you magnify the work of God in your hearts.

2. Pretend you're a veteran mom with your children all grown and out of the house. What battles are you having right now that you need to remember so that you can share God's amazing work of grace in your heart? Write them down, and write down the verses God used to give you victory.

3. Write down a few truths about the realities of new momhood that you wish you had known at the beginning of the journey.

4. Make a list of the ways God has blessed you in your experience as a mother. Spend time praising Him for His goodness.

Yes, 'tis sweet to trust in Jesus,
Just from sin and self to cease.[1]

Louisa M. R. Stead

Chapter Nine

The Battle of Emotions

Just yesterday in the grocery store, I ran into a friend from church I hadn't seen in over a month due to summer travels. We laughed as we hugged each other in greeting, and our children were glad to see their friends too. Within a matter of minutes, tears slid down our faces as we shared grief over another friend whose husband was called home to heaven this week, and our hearts shaken by the pain she is facing. Then our faces lit up in joy contemplating her husband's welcome into the presence of God. In the next minute, we both felt a bit of anxiety as we considered the quickly approaching start of school and all that must be accomplished before then.

We didn't just exchange information in that store aisle. We felt *with* each other. In a ten-minute slice of time, we experienced at least four powerful emotions together and our hearts connected on a deeper, more powerful level. This is one of the beauties of being a woman filled with the Holy Spirit. We are not limited merely to knowing facts. We *feel* them, *taste* them, *live* them. God has granted us the privilege of emotions.

Emotions are highly influential and touch every part of our lives. By providential design, they can be a beautiful expression of God's passion in us. God distinctly created women to experience the depth of existence that emotions provide.

There are hundreds of lists of emotions people are said to experience and multiple levels and interactions between those emotions. Most lists recognize that emotions seem also to have an antithesis, that is, an emotion that is opposite from it. Think through this chart gathered from several theorists and sources.[2]

POSITIVE SIDE OF THE EMOTION	NEGATIVE SIDE OF THE EMOTION
LOVE unselfishness, tenderness	**HATE** selfishness, hostility
JOY happiness, gladness, delight	**SADNESS** sorrow, grief, unhappiness, neglect, rejection
SECURITY peace, rest, relaxation	**FEAR** insecurity, timidity, anxiety, stress, panic, worry
PATIENCE calmness, serenity	**ANGER** rage, disgust
COMPASSION empathy, sympathy, pity, kindness	**CRUELTY** contempt
APPRECIATION gratitude, respect	**ENVY** jealousy, grudging, disrespect
HOPE faith, anticipation	**DESPAIR** depression
MODESTY meekness, mildness, quietness, humility	**PRIDE** arrogance, conceit, immodesty, vanity

See anything you recognize in that list?

> *But the fruit of the Spirit is love, joy, peace, longsuffering, gentleness, goodness, faith, meekness, temperance: against such there is no law.* (Galatians 5:22–23)

Wow! I was stunned and otherworldly happy after doing this study. Secular theorists have identified a collective group of emotions we humans experience. The positive characteristic of each of these major emotion groups is already listed in the Bible as fruit of the Holy Spirit working in our lives.

(By the way, I'm not advocating that you do an in-depth study of secular sources to understand your emotions. The only sincerely valuable observation I gained from doing that study was that the positive manifestation of the major groups of emotions humans experience was already listed in the Bible thousands of years before these theorists were born. And I was once again in awe of my God.)

On a side note, I didn't see anyone list temperance, or self-control, as an emotion. I tend to agree. For a Christian, pure self-control isn't a feeling. It's an act of the will in submission to the Holy Spirit.

All of us experience some form of these emotions—both the positive and negative expressions—multiple times throughout our lives and sometimes even at the same time, as I did in the grocery store aisle.

Emotions are so integrated into our female psyche that it is almost impossible to disconnect them from any situation. Many men have the amazing ability to compartmentalize life experiences so that often their feelings don't strongly affect their job performance. Not always, of course, but a remarkably high percentage of men are able to focus on the task at hand without being distracted or significantly influenced by how they feel about it. This is truly a gift and one I've thought would be wonderful to possess.

We women, on the other hand, were created to see life differently. We were meant not only to live life, but to feel it deeply as well. Emotions are powerful, not a weakness. They are a blessing, not a curse.

They allow us to rejoice fully in good times and grieve profoundly in difficult ones. They can motivate us to action or steel us against action. They add color and beauty to every situation. They allow us to go deeper, higher, further into the moments and the relationships in our lives. They provide for us a brief, albeit finite, glimpse into the passion of the heart of God and the fathomless emotions that are an intricate component of Him. Indeed, even Jesus, in human form, wept at the death of His friend, Lazarus. His tears might have been due in part to the hard unbelief of some of the people observing the scene, but I believe they fell mostly because of the deep grief Lazarus' death caused and perhaps the finality of this separation from a human's point of view. People Jesus loved were hurting. Either way, Jesus wept. Read John 11:1–45 for the entire story.

Matthew 21:11–13 shows Jesus expressing righteous anger at the misuse of His Father's temple by the moneychangers and businessmen. And who can forget the passion and emotion felt and expressed by Jesus in the garden of Gethsemane? Luke 22:39–46 shows that the weight of what was about to happen to Jesus was so heavy and His soul was in such anguish that His physical body began to sweat drops of blood!

Yes, our emotions are an expression of God Himself through our human existence, and we're miraculously created in His image. Emotions are beautiful, that is, when they're under the control of the Holy Spirit in obedience to the Sword. But when allowed to run freely, sinful emotions multiply themselves quickly and without warning. When we permit them to, they overtake us and begin controlling us, dragging us on a downward spiral of destruction. They can be an ugly reminder of the power of sin in our hearts. Out-of-control emotions are deadly. They distort reality, manipulate our motives, and destroy relationships.

With the potential of commanding power like this, don't ever doubt Supermom's efforts to tap into our emotions. If she can dominate them, she can control and influence most of our existence. She's evil. She hates our Creator. It's an incredibly smart move on her part to go after our emotions.

We must be ready.

HORMONE HARMONY

Many factors drive and affect our emotions, including the amount of sleep we get, our season in life, our physical health, and our hormones. Hormones are a God-given part of who we are as individuals. Hormones develop male and female tendencies in our physical and emotional makeup. We just wouldn't be who we are without our hormones.

As with almost everything having to do with our physical bodies, balance is the key to healthy living. Hormones need to be part of that balance.

Contemporary health journals and periodicals publish much about women's health issues these days. Pick up any women's magazine, and you will encounter at least one article or advertisement dealing with women's hormones. It's a big topic. Women are carefully marketed to since they make up the majority of the consumers.

There is no doubt in any woman's mind that after puberty, hormones affect us at least once a month, during pregnancy, during the postpartum period, and during menopause. Among other factors, hormones are affected by your genetics, the medications you take, what you eat, the amount of sleep you get, and your exercise level.

So we have them. And God gave them to us. I confess there are times I've wondered exactly *why* He thought I needed so many of them, but, nevertheless, they are part of me, and I must learn to take my hormones along with me as I walk in the Spirit.

But the glaring question is "How?"

After the birth of my twins, my hormones most certainly lost their state of balance. Combined with a painful recovery from a C-section plus a severe lack of sleep and the physical challenge of establishing milk for two nursing babies, my hormones fluctuated alarmingly. It just wasn't easy for me like Supermom told me it was for everybody else.

I was living in a dark tunnel alone with no end in sight. Oh, I was grateful to have had two healthy babies, and I did love them dearly. But many days and nights I was on autopilot and simply struggled for survival. I met the needs of my children but had little energy for anything else.

My perplexed husband tried to reach out to me on many occasions, but I often simply felt he couldn't possibly understand what I was going through, so without realizing it, I began pushing him away rather than accepting his comfort, falling for the eons-old ploy of Supermom that "no one can possibly understand" me. I felt completely overwhelmed most of the time. Supermom had her hand in that too. She likes isolation.

Hormones don't just affect us emotionally. I had physical manifestations too. During my pregnancies an influx of hormones caused my ligaments to soften to the point I developed carpal tunnel syndrome in my wrists, and the arches in my feet fell, leading to painful heel spurs. When your feet hurt to walk and your fingers are numb and tingly or in pain constantly, it begins to wear down your spirit. (They don't make wrist braces and orthotics for your shoes in designer colors either.)

As I mentioned before, I didn't just skip out on my walk with God during that time. I was in the Word. I prayed often—very often. I had a completely new understanding of what it means in 1 Thessalonians 5:17 to "pray without ceasing," but I still struggled. And I felt like a failure because I was struggling.

Shouldn't a woman who is a Christian just walk in the Spirit and get over it? If she was a real Christian, she wouldn't have these problems, right? Wrong!

Real Christian women who love God, who serve Him faithfully, who are committed to His perfect will for their lives struggle with the depth of their emotions—emotions affected by their hormones! It's part of the curse of Genesis 3. Remember what happened to Eve because she ate the fruit in the Garden of Eden?

> *Unto the woman he [God] said, I will greatly*
> *multiply thy sorrow and thy conception; in sorrow*
> *thou shalt bring forth children; and thy desire shall*
> *be to thy husband, and he shall rule over thee.*
> *(Genesis 3:16)*

There is much speculation on exactly what bringing forth children in sorrow is referring to. Is it just the actual labor and delivery of a child? Does it include the pregnancy stage and the postpartum stage? Or does it include the entire job of carrying, delivering, and rearing a child?

My guess is that it includes the entire process of motherhood from start to finish, every beautiful, painful, precious, frustrating moment of it.

If you're struggling after the birth of a child, say so to your doctor at a postpartum check-up. Communicate your struggle to your husband. Get help from some close, Christian friends. Seek counsel from a pastor and his wife. Above all, don't get trapped by Supermom into isolating yourself! These are the times the body of Christ shines and the world sees Jesus *through* the body in action, demonstrating the love of God by how it ministers to each other.

Ask for and accept offers for help. Reject the idea that you don't want to bother anyone. All of us need help at some point. Wouldn't you reach out to help a friend in need? Let your friends reach out to you.

After the birth of my twins the first week in January, a dear friend took it upon herself to coordinate a month's worth of dinners and grocery shopping trips for me. What love! I was overwhelmed with the care God demonstrated to me through those friends who fed us and did our shopping that dreary, sleepless, cold month in northern Wisconsin. And on top of that, my thoughtful mother-in-law paid a neighbor friend to come over and clean our bathrooms each week. What a blessing! I am eternally grateful.

All too soon the month was over, and I had to go back to cleaning my own bathrooms and making our own meals. And eventually I had to figure out how to shop with three babies. (My secret? Two shopping carts: car seat number one in the back of one cart and the sixteen-month-old strapped in the seat of that cart and car seat number two in the seat of the second cart with groceries in the back of that cart). A single shopping trip also involved a little over an hour of driving time as the closest Walmart Super Center was in the Upper Peninsula of Michigan.

Coordinating shopping trips, diapers, and nursing stops was an exhausting adventure for sure.

Sometime at the end of February, my new reality of three babies under the age of two hit me in the face.

- I was tired.

- This was too hard.

- They cried a lot.

- I was tired.

- My house had a permanent distasteful diaper odor.

- I was tired.

- I felt horrible mom guilt about not spending much quality time with my eldest because of the physical demands of the twins.

- Why wouldn't the twins sleep on the same schedule?

- I was tired.

- And where, exactly, was the glory of momhood?

- Would I ever feel rested again?

- So tired.

THE FLIP SIDE

Let me interject the flip-side of Supermom's tactics here. *I* was tempted to isolate myself with my pain and to be too prideful to accept help from others since it might make me look weak. *You* may struggle with the opposite problem—the spirit of entitlement we talked about earlier. You may accept your position of weakness so entirely that you slide into the pit on the other side of the issue and become lazy. Laziness is dangerous, too, and has destructive power in your relationships within the body of Christ.

If you're lazy, you may not only welcome help from others, but may actually come to expect that help. You could become possessed with the idea that others somehow owe you in your time of need and are obligated to rearrange their busy schedules to accommodate you. This is deep selfishness. Frankly, there are times every mom is exhausted, no matter what her stage of life. Every mom doesn't "feel good" all the time. This is a stark reality we must accept.

God speaks frankly on both sides of the issue.

> *Bear ye one another's burdens, and so fulfil the law of Christ. For if a man think himself to be some-thing, when he is nothing, he deceiveth himself. But let every man prove his own work, and then shall he have rejoicing in himself alone, and not in another. For every man shall bear his own burden.*
> *(Galatians 6:2–5)*

So we will find joy in helping to bear the burden of others when we have the opportunity, but God says to be vigilant. Don't allow ourselves to be deceived into thinking we deserve something from others. Instead we should work hard and prove our own work. We must take our responsibilities seriously and never add to the burden of others through our laziness or poor choices.

A woman filled with the Holy Spirit is thrilled to love her sisters in practical ways, gladly serving when the need arises. But a woman filled with the Holy Spirit never, ever believes that her sisters owe her their service. Please be so careful. Serve faithfully and fully, but never expect to be served. This spirit of entitle-ment leads to laziness that will drain the resources and energy of the Body of Christ.

When God does use His children to bless you in a time of genuine need, give Him the glory and them your sincerest gratitude.

REAL WOMEN

We see the clear evidence of our wonderful female hormones and emotions in the tears, anger, passion, and joy of women in the Bible. What an encouragement these women are to me! I studied these women, their emotions, and their consequences when I was trying to make sense of mine. Here are two women whom God used to change me.

Hannah (1 Samuel 1–2)

Hannah wanted a child. She was one of two wives of a God-fearing man named Elkanah. The Bible says in 1 Samuel 1:5 that "the Lord had shut up her womb."

Her husband's other wife, Peninnah, was evidently not a very nice girl. She found ways and said things to make Hannah's heart ache because she didn't have a child. The Bible says in 1 Samuel 1:6–7 that Peninnah "provoked her sore, for to make her fret, because the Lord had shut up her womb. . . . When she went up to the house of the Lord, so she provoked her."

Even when their family was on the way to worship God, this other wife gave Hannah grief over a circumstance beyond Hannah's control. It broke Hannah's heart and caused her so much pain that "therefore she wept, and did not eat" (1 Samuel 1:7).

Her husband had trouble understanding her problem. Remember he was a God-fearing man who took his family to worship regularly, but he just couldn't figure out why Hannah wasn't happy. I have to smile at his rational-man response to his emotional wife: "Hannah, why weepest thou? and why eatest thou not? and why is thy heart grieved? am not I better to thee than ten sons?" (1 Samuel 1:8).

Nothing is recorded about her immediate reaction to his comment, but I can just imagine the frustration in her heart. Interestingly, the very next thing we know is that after her conversation with her husband, she had a meal and went straight to talk to God about it. That's a good pattern to follow.

She had both emotional and physical manifestations of deep trouble. In fact, she was so emotionally overwrought as she poured out her heart to God in the temple that even the local priest, Eli, assumed she was drunk and confronted her saying, "How long wilt thou be drunken? put away thy wine from thee" (1 Samuel 1:14).

You can be sure that there will be other well-meaning Christians who will misunderstand and misdiagnose *your* emotions and troubles too. Think of Job's three friends who were anything but an encouragement to him.

Sometimes our emotions are out of control and most certainly need to be challenged by God's Word, but sometimes they're legitimate expressions of our heart. Hannah's emotions were deep and powerful, and they were legitimate.

The greatest lesson I learn from Hannah here is that she took her grief and her frustration to one place—her God. She poured out her sorrow to Him! She made a promise to her God that if He would give her a son, she'd give that son right back to Him.

Wow. This is a picture of raw emotion under control. This woman didn't allow her emotions to fuel a selfish desire. Yes, her mother's heart wanted a child to love and care for. But what she wanted *most* was to give of herself to her God through her children.

So God answered her selfless prayer and gave her a son. And Hannah kept her promise to her God. She named her son *Samuel,* which means *asked of God.* As soon as Samuel was old enough to eat solid food, she took him to the temple and gave him into the keeping of Eli to serve the Lord all of his life.

Imagine Hannah's pain of giving up her firstborn child while he was so young, of walking away from him, of completely trusting her toddler to God's care.

We would do well to follow Hannah's example. Our children are not our own. They were not given to us for our glory to satisfy our desires. They are His, and we are merely His stewards of their lives for a very short period of time. His plan for each child far exceeds ours because His love so deeply surpasses ours.

I'm overwhelmed at Hannah's song of praise, the prayer of her heart *after* she walked away from her son. Please take the time to read how she praises her God in 1 Samuel 2:1–10. This was not a sad, bitter woman. This woman was full of genuine joy and prayed a worshipful, full-of-awe prayer about her powerful provider—God!

Every year Hannah visited her son at the temple and brought him a new set of clothing she had made just for him. Her humble character and joyful spirit in the midst of her strong emotions were no doubt a powerful influence in pointing this son of hers to love and fear God. Samuel grew to be a man God used to do mighty things.

And Samuel was very simply the answer to an emotional prayer of a God-loving woman who chose to put her God before herself. We read in 1 Samuel 2:21 that God blessed Hannah with five more children.

Leah (Genesis 29–49:31)

Leah wanted her husband's love, but Jacob loved her sister, Rachel. Sounds like a real-life soap opera, doesn't it?

After Jacob worked for Laban for seven years to earn the hand of his daughter Rachel in marriage, this future father-in-law tricked Jacob into marrying his older daughter, Leah. Can you imagine his rage upon waking up the day after his marriage to discover Leah in his bed, not Rachel? It's a sad story of treachery.

Jacob was so upset that he begged Laban for Rachel. Laban told him that if he'd just finish his wedding celebration to Leah (which lasted a week in that culture), he'd give him Rachel to marry, as long as he also worked another seven years to earn her. Jacob's love for Rachel was so deep that in spite of the obvious betrayal by his father-in-law, he agreed, and Jacob married Rachel just one week after he had married Leah. (Impressive, really, to have your husband love you so much that he would work for fourteen years to win your hand in marriage!)

But what about Leah? She was thrust, most likely without any consent whatsoever, into this marriage by her father. I can't help but think she must have been overwhelmed with grief, grasping the fact that her father thought no man would ever want to marry her and the only way to get rid of her was to trick someone into it. Talk about insecurities. The Bible also says in Genesis 29:17 that Leah was "tender eyed," contrasting that description with Rachel's, saying that Rachel was "beautiful and well favoured." Yup. That would be a bitter pill to swallow.

Leah knew Jacob had been working for her father for the sole purpose of marrying her sister. She knew that Jacob loved her sister, not her. But her father forced her to deceive Jacob and marry him, knowing she was breaking her sister's heart and probably incurring her future husband's contempt.

Our modern feminine sensibilities object strongly to this disrespect and disdain of Laban toward his daughter's feelings. It appears Leah was a pawn to him, nothing more. So how does Leah deal with her reality? She's now locked into a marriage with a man who doesn't love her. Her father obviously doesn't care about her. Her sister is jealous that Leah is the first wife of Jacob.

Actually, not much is said about Leah throughout her life. We do know that God cared about her pain and answered one of the desires of her heart.

> And when the Lord saw that Leah was hated, he opened her womb: but Rachel was barren. (Genesis 29:31)

Perhaps we learn the most of the state of Leah's heart by the names she chose for her first three children—the sons who were such a blessing from God.

> And Leah conceived, and bare a son, and she called his name Reuben: for she said, **Surely the Lord hath looked upon my affliction; now therefore my husband will love me**. And she conceived again, and bare a son; and said, **Because the Lord hath heard that I was hated, he hath therefore given me this son also**: and she called his name Simeon. And she conceived

again, and bare a son; and said, **Now this time will my husband be joined unto me, because I have born him three sons:** *therefore was his name called Levi. (Genesis 29:32–34)*

Go back and consider the names of her sons and the reasons given for her name choices. She's happy about her sons, of course, but they seem to be a means to an end for her, to earn her husband's love.

Leah's story of struggle and competition with her younger sister continues in Genesis 30–34. It's a rather unhappy story that leaves me feeling sad and disturbed when I read it. Her daughter is raped; her sons become murderers. She has to buy her husband's intimacy with mandrakes. There is treachery, deception, and competition among her sons and Rachel's son, Joseph. I'm not sure she ever had her husband's love. There is little mention of Leah's life outside of her desire to earn her husband's love, which seems to have been her life-long quest. Leah was faithful to Jacob all her days, but sadly there isn't concrete evidence that she was actually loved by him.

At her death, Jacob does finally give her a place of honor. She is buried in his family's cemetery plot alongside of Abraham and Sarah, and Isaac and Rebekah, while Scripture records in Genesis 35:19 that Rachel was buried in the desert after dying in childbirth.

So what can I learn from Leah? Although Leah feared the Lord, as was evident by the names of her children, honoring and serving Him was apparently not her heart's highest desire. Her quest for her husband's love was for herself. The woman in me understands her desire. Having your husband's love is a most beautiful gift. But if I allow my emotions to make decisions for me, I will ultimately serve myself. If I desire my husband's love, or my children's love, or anyone's love more than I desire my God, I am setting them up into the position of an idol in my heart. Yes, my emotions can lead me to idolatry.

See how this quest for love—for feeling needed, wanted, esteemed—consumed Leah? Her emotions overtook her spirit and blinded her to the One Person who would have brought her true love and peace—her God. Her emotions craved something that frankly seems right. But those emotions for something good displaced God from her heart. Oh, yes! God was good to her and blessed her with many children, but unlike Hannah whose heart overflowed with praise and love to God for one son, there is no mention that Leah loved her God. She was grateful to God for her children, but gratefulness and love aren't the same.

Gratefulness is simply being thankful and appreciative for something or someone. I can be grateful for someone without truly loving them—like the people who work at the power company. I'm *so* thankful for them and for how they bless me daily with their work. But I don't know them personally, and therefore I don't have the same kind of love in my heart for them as I do for my children. In many forms of true gratefulness, there is still room for selfishness.

Love, on the other hand, is the antithesis of selfishness. I can't truly love someone the way Jesus loves me if I am harboring selfishness in my heart. Most of the time, I'm completely overwhelmed when I try to wrap my head around this kind of love. It's amazing, confusing, and motivating. And from Supermom's point of view, it is impossible.

As for Leah and Hannah, they were two God-fearing women who asked God for help, but for very different reasons. Hannah wanted a child so that she could have yet another avenue to serve God. Leah wanted a child to earn her husband's love. Both asked God. Both asked for good things. But when you get down to the heart of the matter, Hannah's motive was her love of God while Leah's motive was her love for herself.

HEADS OR TAILS?

Motives matter. Motives are the heart of the issue when it comes to discerning how to use our God-given emotions in everyday life.

And, yes, we're supposed to *use* them. We're designed to see life through this beautiful, colorful influence. Too often, I think, in fear of my powerful emotions, I've fallen into the trap of the pendulum swinging in the complete opposite direction: emotions are bad, therefore avoid them at all costs.

I've come to realize that when I say this, I'm audaciously telling my Creator that what He has given me is wrong. No! He has given me good things. Emotions are part of His intended purpose for me as a woman. Please don't fall into that trap. Ignoring your emotions or taping a *sin* sticker over them is just as sinful as allowing them to rule your life.

As I crawled through those early days of momhood, I realized that I needed to deal with my emotions on a new level. Suddenly through hormones, lack of sleep, and babies, my emotions became a very real, in-my-face part of my life. So I tried, Robin-style, to just *do better*, to have more self-control, to not allow my emotions to dominate conversations with my children, husband, and friends. Sometimes it seemed to work; sometimes it didn't. I worked hard to not allow my husband to see me cry. I tried not to yell in anger at my children and to be cheerful in front of my friends. But I noticed that this style of managing my emotions left me feeling a bit dry, dull, and uninterested in life. And that's when I realized that God didn't intend for me to exist without the color of emotion. That was Supermom's trick on me to take away one of God's good gifts to me. She's a thief. I *must* always remember that Supermom doesn't understand true love.

Supermom only operates from selfishness. That self-centered view of life permeates everything she touches. She *is* the spirit of entitlement, thinking that she is owed something by pretty much everyone. She is a master defender of her rights.

When we let her, she will use our emotions to accomplish her life goal, making herself the object of my worship. Her means may vary, but her goal is always the same: to get me to manipulate and control others to meet my own needs for personal gratification and to punish those who don't give it to me when and how I want it. And I fell for her deception time and time again.

So after cycling through multiple failures with my emotions, I pleaded with God for a battle plan to deal with them in a way that brought glory to Him.

Did you catch that? Do you want your emotions under control? Why do you want to control your emotions? At first, I wanted to control my emotions so I could control others' perceptions of me. That was so selfish. No wonder I was failing at it.

Sadly it took me a few years, but I finally realized that my gift of emotion was meant to bring amazing glory to my Creator and to connect me with Him on a deep personal level. It was not meant to be a means of self-gratification.

True help from God came when I pleaded with Him, like Hannah did, to help me so that I could bring glory to Him. It's that simple.

Through His Word and gentle questions, He took me on the journey down to the very motive of my emotions. His questions helped me discern whether an emotion was one that was self-gratifying or God-glorifying.

1. **Why are you angry (or sad, fearful, or some other emotion)?** Usually my answer to this one had to do with me not getting what I wanted. *Sigh*.

2. **What are you trying to communicate when you use this negative emotion in your speech or on your face?** Umm . . . this usually had to do with how I wanted to control, manipulate, or punish someone else for not giving me what I wanted. Yikes.

3. **Do you want your emotions under control?** Well, yes. I don't want to be known as a crazy, irrational, self-centered girl that goes around venting all the time.

4. **And who do you want to control your emotions? You? Or Me?** (This question always struck straight into my heart.) You, Lord. I want you to have control of my emotions. I know that the Spirit is the only one that gives lasting, real fruit. (I learned that lesson well from Chapter 1, right?)

And then the most penetrating question of all for me . . .

5. **And *why* do you want Me to have control of your emotions?** Sadly, often I would have to admit at this

point some selfish reason, much like Leah. I wanted to look spiritual. I wanted to appear like I had it under control. I wanted to be accepted. I wanted someone else to conform to my expectations for them. I wanted to avoid conflict, or some other self-gratifying reason.

That last question was the one Supermom didn't want me to consider. Was I completely, fully, deeply sold-out to bringing glory to my Father? Or was I settling for a more shallow Christianity, a kind of Christian identity where I could bear the name but still pursue my own selfish desires in the guise of spirituality?

Ouch. This one hurt. Yes. I was the self-gratifying girl under the precious blood of Christ with God's eternal forgiveness, but who still wanted to take some of the glory due only to her Savior.

"Why?" questions are penetrating. "Why?" questions from the Word cut to the very marrow of your soul. How I wanted to take the easy way out and avoid the soul searching. I wanted to take Supermom's hand and run with her away from those sharp, pointed questions in my heart. But the Spirit is faithful, just as our Savior and our Father are.

It was during those battles for power over my emotions that I think I began to grasp just a taste of the power of the Holy Spirit. The Spirit draws me, convicts me when I stray, illumines the Word to my heart, and comforts me. Romans 8:26 says the Spirit even gives me the words to say when I can't pray as I should.

The question was, "Why do you want Me to have control of your emotions?" The answer was stunning in its simplicity. How had I missed this again?

So I can abide in Jesus.

That's it. No formulas, no special support groups to attend, no long process to endure. Just abide. Rest. Enjoy. Take pleasure in Jesus.

I started smiling more, praising more, and singing out loud to Him more. Honestly, how could I help it? His joy began bubbling out of me.

In fact the more I rested in Jesus like John 15 says I am supposed to do, the more I recognized the Spirit's work in my heart. He was changing me, giving me an eternal perspective, enlightening me, whispering that He loved me. He begged me to cast my burdens upon Him. He invited me to see my life from His viewpoint. He taught me in love that I could know the truth of Romans 8:28 "that all things work together for good to them that love God, to them who are the called according to his purpose."

In the midst of my exhausted mom-trench, He opened my eyes to catch a glimpse of His good plan for me, a plan that had eternal implications and eternal value for me, for my children.

And after a time, I began to realize that I wasn't having to battle against the sinful manifestations of my emotions as often. Yes, I still have my battles. But seriously! It's not as often as long as I'm abiding in Jesus.

I also realized suddenly one day that this practice of abiding in Jesus had actually freed me to be more emotional—in a good way! My compassion deepened. My sympathy grew. My anger against idolatry and sin increased. I began to see people and events more through the eyes of the Spirit—through the eyes of Jesus—and had the freedom to weep with them, rejoice with them, and just *feel* with them. So in reality, I think I'm on the journey to becoming more deeply emotional, like my Savior is.

I confess my initial response to people in the past was often somewhat critical, measuring them by their appearance, their associations, and their reputation. Making assumptions without knowledge, I didn't see past the surface into their hearts and didn't identify with their pain. I didn't recognize the battles they were facing. And because I didn't see, I couldn't possibly have true compassion or understanding of their hearts just like the Pharisees did to Jesus. They couldn't see anything from God's point of view since they were so full of themselves.

Jesus didn't have the credentials, the connections, the wealth, or even the position of legitimacy by birth. Everyone knew that Mary was expecting Jesus *before* she was actually married. The stigma of His birth followed Him all of His earthly life.

Aren't you amazed that the Creator chose to place Himself within His own creation in such humble circumstances to come save us and to die such a brutal death out of love for us? Yes, this is true love. And love is emptying ourselves of ourselves in humility and being fully filled with the Spirit of God.

This is one reason Jesus became human. He wanted us to know that He understands. He feels with us. He was weary. He was discouraged. He was hungry, thirsty, felt pain. He knew sorrow.

Now when I relate to others, I'm beginning to understand that God wants me first to love them deeply, fully, and emotionally, as He loved me while I was yet a sinner. He wants me to use freely and lavishly His wonderful gift of emotion to give others a glimpse of His love. He wants me to show them Jesus.

WHAT ABOUT ME?

1. On which side of the road does Supermom tempt me to lounge? Is it the side of isolation, rejecting genuine help in my time of genuine need, or the side of laziness, expecting others to expend themselves to accommodate me? Either one damages the body of Christ, throwing in wrenches to slow down its God-designed circuitry. If you find yourself in one of these pits, confess your selfishness and pride, accept God's forgiveness, and restore the relationships He has given to bless you within His church.

2. Who is most in control of your emotions? Supermom or the Holy Spirit?

3. When you consider the examples of Hannah and Leah, which woman do you tend to be most like when it comes to asking God for something? Are you motivated purely by loving your God? Or do you ask Him for His blessings simply to get something you want?

4. How does Supermom tempt you to use your emotions? Make a list of the circumstances and ways she has led you to fail in the past (manipulation of others, punishment for not getting what you want, laziness, etc.)

Write out and memorize the verses you plan to use to resist her when she tempts you again.

5. Are you afraid of expressing the depth of emotion God has given to you, or are you so mastered by your emotions that people see only your emotional displays and not Jesus in you? Consider which side of the road your Supermom tends to lead you. Then spend time resting in Jesus and asking Him to fill you with His heart toward others. It is possible to be a deeply emotional woman whose transparency shows forth only Christ and not herself.

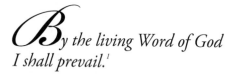

*By the living Word of God
I shall prevail.*[1]

R. Kelso Carter

Chapter Ten
The Battle Plan

Have I fully defeated my Supermom? Nope. Not even close. She rears her ugly head time and time again ready to do battle with the Spirit in me, and battle we do.

The more we battle, the more convinced I am of my weakness and the awesome power of the Word of God and the more I stand amazed that He allows me the awesome privilege of using His Word against the temptations of my sinful nature.

I am convinced that my journey and battles with Supermom won't end with the last chapter of this book. They will persist until God takes me home to heaven. My combat record, my failures, and God-given victories to remember will just continue to grow.

I have no doubt you could add your own chapter to this book. You could write about your own personal battle with whatever sin your Supermom uses to attack you in her quest to bring you pain, make regret a reality in your heart, scream accusations in your ear, and render you useless in bringing others to Jesus. Fight, dear sister. Take seriously your call to be a crusader for Christ.

BATTLE PLAN FOR VICTORY

The longer I fight Supermom, the more methodical I become in dealing with her. The following battle plan is the series of steps I've come to follow when I identify a spiritual battle coming my way.

1. **Rejoice in my standing before God in Christ.** Because I have trusted in Jesus' death on the cross for my sins, the wrath of God is fully satisfied when it comes to me. I can live my life in the peace of God because He loves me and nothing can separate me from that love. I have the Spirit of God within me.

   *And **if Christ be in you, the body is dead because of sin**; but **the Spirit is life** because of righteousness. But if the Spirit of him that raised up Jesus from the dead dwell in you, he that raised up Christ from the dead shall also quicken your mortal bodies by his Spirit that dwelleth in you. Therefore, brethren, we are debtors, not to the flesh, to live after the flesh. For if ye live after the flesh, ye shall die: **but if ye through the Spirit do mortify the deeds of the body, ye shall live.** For as many as are led by the Spirit of God, they are the sons of God. For ye have not received the spirit of bondage again to fear; but **ye have received the Spirit of adoption, whereby we cry, Abba, Father. The Spirit itself beareth witness with our spirit**, that we are the children of God: and if children, then heirs; **heirs of God, and joint-heirs with Christ;** if so be that we suffer with him, that we may be also glorified together. For I reckon that the sufferings of this present time are not worthy to be compared with the **glory which shall be revealed in us.** (Romans 8:10–18)*

   For I am persuaded, that neither death, nor life, nor angels, nor principalities, nor powers,

nor things present, nor things to come, nor
height, nor depth, nor any other creature,
shall be able to separate us from the love
of God, which is in Christ Jesus our Lord.
(*Romans 8:38–39*)

2. **Reflect on the character of God.** He is merciful. He's not out to get me or to condemn me. His condemnation of my sin already happened on the cross of His Son, Jesus, and it is *completed.* God *is* love!

    The Lord is merciful and gracious, slow to
    anger, and plenteous in mercy. He will not always
    chide: neither will he keep his anger for ever.
    He hath not dealt with us after our sins; nor
    rewarded us according to our iniquities. For as
    the heaven is high above the earth, so great is his
    mercy toward them that fear him. As far as the
    east is from the west, so far hath he removed our
    transgressions from us. (*Psalm 103:8–12*)

    God is love. In this was manifested the love of
    God toward us, because that God sent his only
    begotten Son into the world, that we might live
    through him. Herein is love, not that we loved
    God, but that he loved us, and sent his Son to
    be the propitiation for our sins. (*1 John 4:8–10*)

3. **Remember I am free from sin.** I owe Supermom nothing. Because Jesus has defeated her and I have accepted His sacrifice for me, she has no power over me except that which I give to her. Now I can live in the grace of God, not in bondage to my sin.

    Know ye not, that so many of us as were baptized
    into Jesus Christ were baptized into his death?
    Therefore we are buried with him by baptism
    into death: that like as Christ was raised up
    from the dead by the glory of the Father, even so
    we also should walk in newness of life. For if
    we have been planted together in the likeness of

his death, we shall be also in the likeness of his resurrection: knowing this, that our old man is crucified with him, that the body of sin might be destroyed, **that henceforth we should not serve sin. For he that is dead is freed from sin.** *Now if* **we be dead with Christ,** *we believe that* **we shall also live with him***: knowing that Christ being raised from the dead dieth no more;* **death hath no more dominion over him.** *For in that he died, he died unto sin once: but in that he liveth, he liveth unto God. Likewise* **reckon** *ye also* **yourselves to be dead indeed unto sin,** *but alive unto God through Jesus Christ our Lord.* **Let not sin therefore reign in your mortal body,** *that ye should obey it in the lusts thereof. Neither yield ye your members as instruments of unrighteousness unto sin:* **but yield yourselves unto God,** *as those that are alive from the dead, and your members as instruments of righteousness unto God. For sin shall not have dominion over you:* **for ye are not under the law, but under grace.** *(Romans 6:3–14)*

There is therefore now no condemnation to them which are in Christ Jesus, *who walk not after the flesh, but after the Spirit. For the law of the Spirit of life in* **Christ Jesus hath made me free from the law of sin** *and death. (Romans 8:1–2)*

4. **Don't be surprised by trials and temptations.** Everyone that belongs to Jesus has them, just like He had them. I am not alone. I am not exempt. I will have the fellowship of the sufferings of my Savior in my journey to become more like Him.

Beloved, **think it not strange concerning the fiery trial which is to try you,** *as though some strange thing happened unto you:* **but rejoice,**

*inasmuch as **ye are partakers of Christ's sufferings**; that, when his glory shall be revealed, ye may
be glad also with exceeding joy. (1 Peter 4:12–13)*

*My brethren, count it all joy when ye fall into
divers temptations; knowing this, that the trying of
your faith worketh patience. But let patience have
her perfect work, that ye may be perfect and entire,
wanting nothing. (James 1:2–4)*

*Yea, and **all that will live godly** in Christ Jesus
shall suffer persecution. (2 Timothy 3:12)*

*There hath no temptation taken you but such as is
common to man. (1 Corinthians 10:13)*

*For we have not an high priest [**Jesus**] which cannot be touched with the feeling of our infirmities;
but **was in all points tempted like as we are,
yet without sin**. Let us therefore **come boldly**
unto the throne of grace, that we may **obtain
mercy**, and **find grace to help in time of need**.
(Hebrews 4:15–16)*

5. **Reject the blame game**. Acknowledge where my sin
   comes from—*me*—, not from others, not from God,
   and not from a set of circumstances beyond my control.
   I choose how I will respond in every situation. Consider
   the depth and depravity of my sin and my sinful nature
   —Supermom. Remember I am drawn away from God
   by my own lust for self. My consequences are my own.

   *Let no man say when he is tempted, I am tempted
   of God: for **God cannot be tempted with evil,
   neither tempteth he any man**: but **every man**
   is tempted, when he **is drawn away of his own
   lust**, and enticed. Then **when lust hath con-
   ceived, it bringeth forth sin**: and **sin**, when it is
   finished, **bringeth forth death**. (James 1:13–15)*

The heart is deceitful above all things, and desperately wicked: who can know it? (Jeremiah 17:9)

6. **Remember that God knows I am weak and will never allow me to be tempted beyond what I am able to handle with His help.** He knows I cannot do anything without Him. He stands ready to help. I couldn't save myself from the eternal consequences of my sin, and I cannot battle and defeat my current temptations without Him either.

Like as a father pitieth his children, so the Lord pitieth them that fear him. For he knoweth our frame; he remembereth that we are dust. (Psalm 103:13–14)

There hath no temptation taken you but such as is common to man: but God is faithful, who will not suffer you to be tempted above that ye are able; but will with the temptation also make a way to escape, that ye may be able to bear it. (1 Corinthians 10:13)

7. **Remember this battle is a spiritual one.** The battle is within our hearts, for our hearts. My weapons to win are also spiritual.

Thou therefore endure hardness, as a good soldier of Jesus Christ. (2 Timothy 2:3)

For though we walk in the flesh, we do not war after the flesh: (For the weapons of our warfare are not carnal, but mighty through God to the pulling down of strong holds.) (2 Corinthians 10:3–4)

8. **Rejoice that God has given me every single thing I need to defeat Supermom.** Everything.

For God hath not given us the spirit of fear; but of power, and of love, and of a sound mind. (2 Timothy 1:7)

*But continue thou in the things which thou hast learned and hast been assured of, knowing of whom thou hast learned them; and that from a child thou hast known the holy scriptures, which are able to make thee wise unto salvation through faith which is in Christ Jesus. **All scripture is given by inspiration of God, and is profitable for doctrine, for reproof, for correction, for instruction in righteousness: that the man of God may be** perfect, **thoroughly furnished unto all good works**. (2 Timothy 3:14–17)*

9. **The Word of God is powerful.** Satan can't stand against it.

   ***Every word of God is pure: he is a shield** unto them that put their trust in him. (Proverbs 30:5)*

   *The words of the **Lord** are pure words: as silver tried in a furnace of earth, purified seven times. (Psalm 12:6)*

   *The grass withereth, the flower fadeth: but **the word of our God shall stand for ever**. (Isaiah 40:8)*

   ***Man shall** not **live by** bread alone, but by **every word that proceedeth out of the mouth of God**. (Matthew 4:4)*

   ***For the word of God is quick**, and **powerful**, and **sharper than any twoedged sword**, piercing even to the dividing asunder of soul and spirit, and of the joints and marrow, **and is a discerner of the thoughts and intents of the heart**. (Hebrews 4:12)*

   *I have written unto you, young men, because ye are strong, and the **word of God abideth in you**, and **ye have overcome the wicked one**. (1 John 2:14)*

10. **Prepare for battle**. Memorize specific battle plan verses, especially in areas I know I am tempted.

*Who is this King of glory? The **Lord** strong and mighty, the **Lord** mighty in battle. (Psalm 24:8)*

*When the wicked, even mine enemies and my foes, came upon me to eat up my flesh, they stumbled and fell. Though an host should encamp against me, my heart shall not fear: **though war should rise against me, in this will I be confident. One thing have I desired of the Lord**, that will I seek after; **that I may dwell in the house of the Lord** all the days of my life, **to behold the beauty of the Lord**, and to enquire in his temple. (Psalm 27:2–4)*

11. **Cry out for divine help.** At the first sign of a temptation, petition the throne of God for help in fighting this battle. This is taking up my shield of faith.

*The horse is prepared against the day of battle: but safety is of the **Lord**. (Proverbs 21:31)*

__Make haste, O God, to deliver me__; make haste to help me, O Lord. (Psalm 70:1)

*But I am poor and needy: make haste unto me, O God: thou art my help and my deliverer; O **Lord**, make no tarrying. (Psalm 70:5)*

*For the Lord **God** will help me; therefore shall I not be confounded: therefore have I set my face like a flint, and I know that I shall not be ashamed. (Isaiah 50:7)*

12. **Fight.** After asking for God's help, begin quoting His Word to myself. Say it again. Say it out loud. Bring my mind into captivity.

__Blessed be the Lord my strength, which teacheth my hands to war, and my fingers to fight__. (Psalm 144:1)

Fight the good fight of faith. (1 Timothy 6:12)

*Submit yourselves therefore **to God. Resist the devil, and he will flee** from you. **Draw nigh to God**, and **he will draw nigh to you**.* (James 4:7–8)

13. **Expect to do battle with the same temptation again.** And again. And again. Our temptations will be stronger and last longer when they're in an area we've indulged in or where we habitually sin. For example, the longer I have lived in a spirit of fear, the longer I can expect to fight that temptation before I begin to see the attacks lessen in number and/or duration. The attacks will never fully stop while we're here on the earth, but the more we run to God and use His Word in our battles, the less often Supermom bothers to tempt us in that area. She really hates it when we run to God for help.

*For **a just man falleth** seven times, **and riseth up again**.* (Proverbs 24:16)

***Many are the afflictions of the righteous: but the Lord delivereth him** out of them all.* (Psalm 34:19)

***Confess your faults one to another**, and pray one for another, that ye may be healed. The effectual fervent prayer of a righteous man availeth much.* (James 5:16)

*My little children, these things write I unto you, that ye sin not. And **if any man sin, we have an advocate with the Father, Jesus Christ the righteous**.* (1 John 2:1)

***If we say that we have no sin, we deceive ourselves**, and the truth is not in us. **If we confess our sins, he is faithful and just to forgive us our sins**, and to cleanse us from all unrighteousness.* (1 John 1:8–9)

14. **After the battle, remember.** Remember my weakness. Write it down. Then remember and write down what I know about the power of God and how He delivered me from that temptation. Record the verses He used to defeat the temptations of Supermom.

   And thou shalt remember all the way which **the Lord thy God led thee** *these forty years in the wilderness,* **to humble thee,** *and* **to prove thee,** *to know what was in thine heart, whether thou wouldest keep his commandments, or no. (Deuteronomy 8:2)*

   Remember his marvellous works *that he hath done,* **his wonders, and the judgments of his mouth.** *(1 Chronicles 16:12)*

   And **they remembered that God was their rock, and the high God their redeemer.** *(Psalm 78:35)*

15. **I am accountable.** I will give an account of myself to God. I will have the opportunity one day to come face to face with my Father and will be held responsible for how I used the time He gave me here on the earth, for how I faced my sin, for what I did with temptation, and for how I handled the Sword He has so graciously given me as His beloved child. Was I lazy? Was I faithful? Was I complacent? Was I zealous? Did my Sword get rusty from disuse? Or did I keep it clean, sharp, and ready for battle?

   So then **every one** *of us* **shall give account of himself to God.** *(Romans 14:12)*

CALL TO ARMS

This battle plan is the one I follow. At the end of this short life here on finite earth, my heart's desire is to kneel before my Savior and say like Paul did, "I have fought a good fight, I have finished my course, I have kept the faith" (2 Timothy 4:7).

And because I passionately love Him, I want more than anything to hear Him reply, "Well done, good and faithful servant" (Matthew 25:23).

I challenge you to think through and write down your battle plan. Print it out. Post it in a prominent place when you face a battlefield of temptation and see your Supermom looming over you ready to attack. Go through these steps out loud. Memorize the verses and speak them out loud to your heart. So what if your children hear you doing battle with your sin? You're training them to fight too. Do everything you can to be an example of a soldier of Christ to them.

I beg you never to avoid a battle with Supermom. Fight her. Don't cower or ignore her attacks. Don't succumb to her sweet whispers for complacency or settle for a weak Christianity that knows nothing of the power of God. Don't make peace with her. Don't avoid conflict because it's too humbling or too painful. If you do, she will rob you of joy. No, she can't touch your eternal soul or bring you eternal consequences, but here in *this* life, she can lead you to suffer the harsh consequences of sinful choices. Or even worse, she can seduce you with self-righteousness, leading you to walk a life of insecurity by doubting God's love for you.

While I'm here on this earth, I'm pretty sure I will revisit tattered battlefields I once counted as victories. I most assuredly will face new, deeper and darker battlefields within my heart. But I can say this with profound, peaceful conviction:

- I am not alone. I'm abiding in Jesus. This battle is His.

- And God's Word will prevail every time. Every single time.

If we take the time to battle Supermom for the glory of God, we will see the beauty of victory God's Word brings to our lives. We will catch a glimpse of the undercurrents of God's love and overarching plan He has for us. God has a beautiful, fulfilling eternal design for me and for you.

> *For I know the thoughts that I think toward you,*
> *saith the Lord, thoughts of peace, and not of evil,*
> *to give you an expected end. (Jeremiah 29:11)*

With absolute conviction, we can live, "Being confident of this very thing, that he which hath begun a good work in you will perform it until the day of Jesus Christ" (Philippians 1:6). And truly "If God be for us, who can be against us?" (Romans 8:31).

My dear sister-in-the-trenches with me, pursue Jesus. Rest in Jesus. He is so worth it! I want you more than anything "**to know the love of Christ**." (See Ephesians 3:19). You will be overwhelmed in His love.

WHAT ABOUT ME?

1. What is your battle plan? Write out the steps you want to take to win your battle with your Supermom the next time she attacks you. Support each of your steps with at least one Bible verse. Remember, it's not a clever battle plan that wins the fight. It's the Word of God that has the power to defeat Supermom.

2. Choose a spiritual battle topic you are most likely to face soon (pride, selfishness, anger, etc.). Write out and memorize the battle verses you need to be ready to fight that battle. **Post** them somewhere obvious where they cannot be ignored.

3. Communicate your battle plan to your husband and/ or children. Ask them to pray for you as you pursue victory over your Supermom!

   Choose at least one other woman in a similar stage of life as you are who will join you in this battle against Supermom. Keep each other accountable. Pray for and with one another even if it's over the phone or Internet. Share your victories and defeats. Encourage each other with the Word.

Appendix

These verses are meant to be memorized to keep you razor sharp and ready for battle. At the first sign of temptation, let the Word of God rush out of your heart, roll through your mind and right off the tip of your tongue. Supermom can't fight back for long.

These fighting truths from Scripture relate to topics discussed in this book. Sometimes there is an entire verse, and sometimes there is only the part of the verse that focuses your mind on the powerful truth relevant to each topic. The verses are purposely broken into segments to make them easier to memorize.

These temptations are listed alphabetically. This is only a tiny sampling from the powerful Sword handed to you by God for your defense. You probably need to choose the topics and verses from this chart that you need and then add more of your own temptations and the correlating battle verses to your own chart.

Warrior moms memorize God's Word. The battle is fierce. The battle is real. Be ready.

ANGER

James 1:20 The wrath of man worketh not the righteousness of God.

Ecclesiastes 7:9 Be not hasty in thy spirit to be angry: for anger resteth in the bosom of fools.

Colossians 3:21 Fathers, provoke not your children to anger, lest they be discouraged.

COMMON BATTLES

1 Peter 5:8–9 Be sober, be vigilant;
Because your adversary the devil, as a roaring lion, walketh about, seeking whom he may devour:
Whom resist stedfast in the faith,
knowing that the same afflictions are accomplished in your brethren that are in the world.

1 Corinthians 10:13 There hath no temptation taken you but such as is common to man:
but God is faithful,
who will not suffer you to be tempted above that ye are able;
but will with the temptation also make a way to escape that ye may be able to bear it.

CONTENTMENT

1 Timothy 6:6 But godliness
with contentment
is great gain.

Philippians 4:11*b* I have learned,
in whatsoever state I am,
therewith to be
content.

Hebrews 13:5*b* Be content with such things as ye have:
for he hath said,
I will never leave thee, nor forsake thee.

Philippians 1:6 Being confident of this very thing,
that he which hath begun a good work in you
will perform it
until the day of Jesus Christ.

EMOTION

Psalm 126:5 They that sow in tears
shall reap in joy.

Proverbs 16:20 He that handelth a matter wisely shall find good:
and whoso trusteth in the Lord,
happy is he.

Proverbs 17:22 A merry heart doeth good like a medicine:
but a broken spirit drieth the bones.

Hebrews 4:15 For we have not an high priest [Jesus]
which cannot be touched with
the feeling of our infirmities;
but was in all points tempted like as we are,
yet without sin.

EXPECTATIONS

1 Corinthians 4:2 It is required in stewards,
that a man be found faithful.

Micah 6:8 He hath shewed thee, O man, what is good;
and what doth the Lord require of thee,
but to do justly,
and to love mercy,
and to walk humbly with thy God?

2 Corinthians 10:12*b* But they measuring themselves by themselves,
and comparing themselves among themselves,
are not wise.

FEAR

Proverbs 18:10 The name of the Lord is a strong tower:
the righteous runneth into it,
and is safe.

Proverbs 21:31 The horse is prepared against the day of battle:
but safety is of the Lord.

2 Timothy 1:7 For God hath not given us the spirit of fear;
but of power,
and of love,
and of a sound mind.

2 Corinthians 12:9a My grace is sufficient for thee:
for my strength is made perfect in weakness.

Psalm 121:7 The Lord shall preserve thee from all evil:
he shall preserve thy soul.

INSECURITY (POSITION IN CHRIST)

2 Corinthians 5:17 Therefore if any man be in Christ, he is a new creature:
old things are passed away;
behold, all things are become new.

Ephesians 2:19 Now therefore ye are no more strangers and foreigners,
but fellowcitizens with the saints,
and of the household of God.

Romans 8:16–17a The Spirit itself beareth witness with our spirit,
that we are the children of God:
And if children, then heirs;
heirs of God,
and joint-heirs with Christ;

Romans 8:37–39 Nay, in all these things we are more than conquerors
through him that loved us.
For I am persuaded, that neither death, nor life,
nor angels, nor principalities, nor powers,
nor things present, nor things to come,
nor height, nor depth, nor any other creature,
shall be able to separate us from
the love of God, which is in Christ Jesus our Lord.

Romans 8:31*b* If God be for us, who can be against us?

LAZINESS

Proverbs 18:9 He also that is slothful in his work
is brother to him that is a great waster.

Proverbs 19:15 Slothfulness casteth into a deep sleep;
and an idle soul shall suffer hunger.

Proverbs 20:4 The sluggard will not plow by reason of the cold;
therefore shall he beg in harvest,
and have nothing.

THE MIND

2 Timothy 1:7 For God hath not given us the spirit of fear;
but of power,
and of love,
and of a sound mind.

Romans 8:6 For to be carnally minded is death;
but to be spiritually minded
is life and peace.

2 Corinthians 10:5 Casting down imaginations,
and every high thing that exalteth itself
against the knowledge of God,
and bringing into captivity
every thought
to the obedience of Christ.

Philippians 4:8 Finally, brethren, whatsoever things are true,
whatsoever things are honest,
whatsoever things are just,
whatsoever things are pure,
whatsoever things are lovely,
whatsoever things are of good report;
if there be any virtue, and if there be any praise,
think on these things.

PRIDE

Romans 7:18*a* For I know that in me
(that is, in my flesh,)
dwelleth no good thing.

Proverbs 16:18 Pride goeth before destruction,
and an haughty spirit
before a fall.

James 4:6*b* God resisteth the proud,
but giveth grace
unto the humble.

Philippians 2:3 Let nothing be done through strife or vainglory;
but in lowliness of mind
let each esteem other
better than themselves.

SELFISHNESS

Philippians 2:3–4 Let nothing be done through strife or vainglory;
but in lowliness of mind
let each esteem other better than themselves.
Look not every man on his own things,
but every man also on the things of others.

Galatians 6:2–3 Bear ye one another's burdens,
and so fulfil the law of Christ.
For if a man think himself to be something,
when he is nothing,
he deceiveth himself.

Proverbs 18:17 He that is first in his own cause seemeth just;
but his neighbor cometh and searcheth him.

Proverbs 3:27 Withhold not good to them from whom it is due,
when it is in the power of thine hand to do it.

THE SWORD

Proverbs 30:5   Every word of God is pure:
he is a shield unto them that
put their trust in him.

Matthew 4:4*b*   Man shall not live by bread alone,
but by every word that proceedeth
out of the mouth of God.

Hebrews 4:12   For the word of God is quick, and powerful,
and sharper than any twoedged sword,
piercing even to the dividing asunder of soul and spirit,
and of the joints and marrow,
and is a discerner
of the thoughts and intents
of the heart.

Endnotes

CHAPTER 1

1. George Duffield, Jr. "Stand Up, Stand Up for Jesus," 1858.

CHAPTER 2

1. Charles Wesley, "Soldiers of Christ, Arise," 1749.

CHAPTER 3

1. Amy Carmichael, *If.* (Fort Washington, PA: Christian Literature Crusade, 1984), 66.

CHAPTER 4

1. Howard A. Walter, "I Would Be True," 1906.

CHAPTER 5

1. Aaron R. Wolfe, "Complete in Thee," 1858.

2. Emily Jordan, "Of Glory," http://batteragainstthebrilliance. blogspot.com/2012/03/of-glory.html.

CHAPTER 6

1. Arthur G. Bennett. Ed. Valley of Vision, (Carlisle, PA: Banner of Truth, 2002), 84.

2. Carmichael, 59.

CHAPTER 7

1. A. A. Fitzgerald Whiddington, "Not I, but Christ," 1891.

2. C. S. Lewis. *Screwtape Letters,* (New York: HarperCollins, 2001), 12.

CHAPTER 8

1. John Newton, "Amazing Grace," 1829.

CHAPTER 9

1. Louisa M. R. Stead, " 'Tis So Sweet to Trust in Jesus," 1882.

2. A. Ortony and T. J. Turner, "What's basic about basic emotions?" *Psychological Review* 97 (1990): 315–31.; W. Parrott, W., *Emotions in Social Psychology,* (Philadelphia: Psychology Press, 2001). Aristotle quoted in R. Plutchik and H. Kellerman, eds., *Emotion, Theory, research, and experience.* (New York: Academic, 1980), 1:3–33.

CHAPTER 10

1. R. Kelso Carter, "Standing on the Promises," 1886.